# GOD

# IS

# BIGGER

# GOD
# IS
# BIGGER

### His Amazing Rescue from Abuse, Addiction, PTSD, Divorce, and Despair

Curtis Brown
with
David Gregory

*Narwhal Press*

Published by Narwhal Press
Magnolia, Texas
www.narwhalpress.com

Published in the United States of America
ISBN 978-0-9971941-7-3
10 9 8 7 6 5 4 3 2 1

# CONTENTS

# PART ONE

# MY STORY

CHAPTER 1

# THE SHOES WE WALK IN

As a young child I was virtually unable to hear, unable to talk right, and unable to walk without losing my balance and falling over. Given the other things I ended up facing in life, those issues seem pretty minor.

At the start, at least, my life would have been a bit easier if I had born today. I was born prematurely on July 21, 1967, in Martinez, California. I had serious ear defects and a poorly functioning immune system.

My ear problems came from Eustachian tubes that weren't fully developed. Excess fluid buildup that was supposed to drain down the back of my throat couldn't drain because the tubes were closed off. This put enough pressure directly on my eardrums that they would burst. Before I was six months old, doctors started putting in artificial tubes. But that technology was a long way from being perfected in 1967.

Pressure in my eardrums caused chronic pain, chronic ear infections, and very restricted hearing. I could hear some sounds at times, but most of the time, I could barely hear at all.

My hearing problem created many other challenges. Our

balance originates in our inner ear, and mine was all off. I couldn't walk without running into things or falling. I'm sure when I was learning to walk it was a comical thing to see. I had many bumps and bruises and even black eyes from not being able to keep my balance or walk straight. My poor mother couldn't keep any decorations or breakables within my reach.

My dad constantly spanked me as a result of my hearing impairment. He would get mad because I wouldn't react to him when he called me. Many years later he asked for my forgiveness. He said he didn't realize how little I could hear him.

My hearing problem also created a speech impediment, or what seemed to be one. Actually, I could have spoken just fine. I just couldn't hear, and if you can't hear, you don't learn to speak right.

Around age six I started to hear better. I guess my tubes finally formed correctly. Or the artificial ones started working right. I don't know. By age eight or nine my balance got much better, as did my speech.

But the ability to hear was a mixed blessing. The world, I discovered, can be a cruel place for those who hear. I realized that many people weren't happy like I usually was. I could now hear people making fun of how I talked, and teasing me about falling down all the time.

Before my hearing returned all the way, while I was in kindergarten in California, school officials put me in a special education class because I would not communicate with them the way they thought that I should. To capture my attention, you had to look me straight in the eye and speak to me. Then I would respond. But the teachers and administrators didn't know this, because they didn't know me, nor did they try to examine me to find out about my handicap.

I found this incredibly discouraging. To me, they didn't

seem to care. *All they have to do is contact my parents and ask them what is wrong with me and how they can communicate with me*, I would think. That would have been so easy. My mother worked for the school so she was already on campus. If they had cared enough about me, they could have walked across campus and asked her what was wrong with me. But because they didn't understand my disability, they labeled me as mentally retarded.

When my mother found this out, she was very upset. She immediately she came to my class and brought the principal with her. "Please watch," Mom said to her.

Mom looked me straight in the eye and spoke to me, and though I could hear somewhat better by then, I mostly read lips because of habit. Mom said, "Curtis, count to 100 for me," and I did. Mom then said, "Curtis, tell me your ABCs," and I did that as well. The principal and the teacher were amazed. They had no idea that I was actually smart.

Unless we have walked in someone else's shoes, it's hard to relate to them. We can sympathize, which is important, but we don't really know what it's like to go through what they are going through. The school officials just didn't understand what I was going through.

I guess you could say that I've walked in a lot of people's shoes. I've endured physical and emotional abuse and alcoholism growing up, a gun to the head, my best buddy being killed in war, severe military injuries, endless surgeries, debilitating chronic pain, addiction to pain medications, post-traumatic stress disorder, sex addiction, alcohol abuse, divorce, and the consequences of one bad decision after another.

I tried to find fulfillment and freedom in a bottle, in drugs, in material things, in sexual videos, and in bed with women. I found that none of them fulfilled, and none of them could set me free.

I lived for many years thinking that I could never be forgiven for all the bad things I had done. I truly believed that I had messed up so bad with the horrible choices that I had made in my life that God didn't want anything to do with me anymore.

But I learned that that was a lie. God brought me through it all, healed me, healed my family, and set our lives on a course of great blessing.

One day, my son Micah approached me as I was starting to write this book. He said, "Dad, I know why you are writing this book."

I replied, "Tell me, Son, why am I writing this book?"

Micah answered, "You're writing this book so people will see that God loves them no matter what they've done wrong in their lives."

He hit the nail on the head. If anyone's life shows that God still loves us, that He forgives, that He heals, and that He restores hope, mine does.

That's where we all have been, haven't we? Needing love, needing forgiveness, needing healing, needing hope. Those are the shoes I've walked in. And now, in a small way, I walk into your life, you who have opened this book. I come with a story of great hope.

*CHAPTER 2*

# PROGRAMMED TO SELF-DESTRUCT

My mom and dad were both originally from Oklahoma. My dad was born in Shawnee and my mother in Stuart. My dad's parents moved to California for work, and my mother moved to California to live with her oldest sister when she was a teenager. Her sister lived right next to my dad's parents' house, which is how they met.

Being the youngest child and having health issues meant that I was at home a lot. I was watched mostly by my dad. For most kids this might be a good thing. For me it wasn't. My siblings and I endured daily emotional abuse and frequent physical abuse. Dad was a perfect example of what people mean when they say, "Hurt people hurt people." He was angry and abusive throughout my childhood and into my late teenage years.

I lived my childhood and teenage life fearing that I might make a wrong move around my dad, which in turn would cause him to get angry. No one in our home ever wanted to make my dad angry. My dad was like a tyrant in our home. I know what it's like to be a tyrant. Later in life, in some ways, I became the very things that I hated the most in my dad as I was growing up. Hurt people hurt people.

I thank God that He did give me several adventures which were my way of escaping from reality.

When I was very young, I learned that the best way of escaping the turmoil in our household was to go toad frog hunting every morning. If I got up early and walked down the sidewalk and lifted the lids of water meters, I could catch toad frogs before anyone caught me. We lived in Shore Acres at the time, which was near San Francisco Bay. I was four or five. Every day, I would set my mental alarm clock, get out of bed, don my hunting gear (underwear and a T-shirt) and be off on my hunting expedition. I had to perform each movement in stealth mode to get out onto the carport (my hunting outpost) without being detected. While on my mission, I approached the toad frogs in stealth mode as well so that they would not be alerted. I was able to use the man-made traps (water meter boxes) to my advantage. The toad frogs would get trapped inside the water meters while searching for food. This created a perfect opportunity for me to catch them. My escape from our household reality was achieved.

I didn't just go into stealth mode for frog hunting. I had to go in stealth mode daily to attempt to prevent any altercation with my dad. Although I had a constant fear of being whipped by him, I also had a desire for his love and acceptance. I always dreamed of having a dad like some of the dads on the television. I was captured by the father figures on television shows like *The Waltons* or *Little House on the Prairie*. I just wanted my dad to hold me and be a father to me, to show me love and do things with me. As I look back at my childhood, it's still easy for tears to fall.

At our house, we were bound by rules which were strictly enforced. But the rules changed every day depending on Dad's mood. He was like a dictator, seeking to find any excuse to enforce his own rules. My brother Dewayne and I could just be wrestling around, which might be fine today, but tomorrow, Dad might beat us for doing the same thing. In our home, the atmosphere changed from second to second, and you never knew when the storm was coming. You just knew that there was going to be a storm. I would try to escape or avoid my dad by staying in my bedroom while my siblings were at school and my mom was at work. I was literally scared to death of my dad. It breaks my heart to think about those days.

Fortunately, the painful times we had to endure were leavened with fun times and good memories as well. On Saturday mornings my brother Dewayne and I would get up early so we could watch cartoons. There was a competition between Dewayne and I to see who got up the earliest. Whoever woke up earliest chose which cartoons we would view. This went on for many years, and I will always cherish the time we spent together.

Even through the many trials and brokenness in our home, Dewayne and I were able to overcome by the ability God gave us to bring our imaginations to reality. We built, we played and we explored on a daily basis. Dewayne and I are very close to this day, and I thank God regularly for the relationship that He has given me with my brother, and with all my siblings. I have many special memories that I truly cherish with both my oldest brother Jerry Allen and my sister Carla. I believe that we are all so close because we realized how much we needed each other while we were young. Though at times we would argue and fight, deep down there is a love and bond that God created that can't be broken.

While I was growing up, my dad spent most of his time lying on the couch watching television. He indulged in what the world offered him for escape: TV, porn, cigarettes, alcohol, violent movies and/or cartoons and even some video games.

Dad made us go to Sunday school and church, but he would only go with us once a year, on Easter, and sometimes he wouldn't go even then. Dad always told me that he had his own personal relationship with Jesus Christ, yet he would never read the Bible, and he didn't live like a Christian man. We attended Shore Acres Baptist Church, and my mother was faithful to take us to Sunday school and church every week. Actually, I loved the church, and I had many friends who went there with their families.

I wasn't quite two when my dad was in a bad 18-wheeler accident which drastically changed his life. He sustained serious injuries which impaired his ability to work afterward.

Before Dad's accident, we were on our way to living a very comfortable life. Dad owned a couple of big rig trucks and trailers and a full-service gas station that were all doing very well. After the accident, he was unable to keep the trucking business going, and things beyond his control caused him to lose the gas station.

I had no way of knowing this at the time, of course, but having had the same experience as an adult, I can see now how this episode affected his life. I believe that after this Dad lost his way. When a man gets injured to the point that it alters his ability to work and support his family, it seems to change everything. My dad sought relief in various ways, all of them unhealthy.

Sadly, Dad started punishing his family for what happened to him. I always dreamed of a real father figure and not a just a man who resided in our home. As a young child, I didn't truly understand what I was seeking or desiring, but I just knew that I was sad and lonely. I didn't even understand why my dad was always so angry and why his moods constantly changed. I realize now that I was longing for acceptance and searching for someone to love me and lead me. God had placed my dad in our family to do that, but somewhere down the road, he got off track, and it created tremendous damage in our home and in our lives.

Many of the images burned into my mind from that time come from my dad being addicted to pain medications and alcohol, a bad combination. I can still see my dad standing in the bathroom giving injections to himself. This memory is very vivid because I had a huge fear of needles from the painful gamma-globulin and penicillin shots I got regularly.

The sad part is that Dad did not just stop at the injections. After Dad gave himself the shots, he would take several pills and later on he would add alcohol. I truly wish the doctors as well as the pharmaceutical companies would have seen the monster that they had created. Even though I was young, I could put two and two together.

The shots made my dad meaner. Adding the pills and the alcohol meant a whole day in stealth mode for me. I just hoped Dad would fall asleep and not wake up until someone else got home. I can remember a few times that my great grandpa (we called him Clon-Daddy) came by and saved the day for me.

Because Dad was always on edge, we were always walking on egg shells. Dad was so unhappy and angry, and he constantly took his hurt out on us, constantly yelling at us while putting us down and whipping us and not knowing when to stop. He would often send us to our room for hours upon hours while telling us that he would be in there soon to whip us. When Dad did this, which was pretty often, I would do my best to stay out of his sight as well as try not to make any noise.

## CHAPTER 3

## TRIALS AND SMILES

Looking back at my childhood, however, I can remember times that my dad showed genuine love and compassion. One morning, Dad was called to come down the street to help deliver some puppies for some neighbor friends. They had Chihuahua dogs that they bred and sold. One puppy came out but was not breathing, and Dad actually gave the puppy CPR and revived her. They gave Dad the puppy; he named her Nina.

Dad, Mom, Carla and Jerry Allen helped nurse the puppy, and Nina thrived and grew up to be a family pet for many years. Nina loved to sleep in bed with all of us, and it sometimes caused arguments over who got to let her sleep with them. Nina also loved to sleep in the clothes basket. One day, she got into the dirty clothes basket and buried herself in it. Mom put the clothes in the washer. A little while later the washer was off balance and Mom opened up the lid to rearrange the clothes. Mom screamed, "A rat's in the washer! A rat's in the washer!" She then realized that it was Nina. She got her out and dried her off and tried to comfort her. But Nina was scared to death. It took months before Nina would have anything to do with

Mom again!

Dad's acts of kindness to others, but not to his own family, confused me. I didn't know who he really was or what he really stood for and believed. I was proud to be his son when he did these kind things, but why didn't he do them for us? One funny story arose from the things that Dad did. He literally turned our small neighborhood home and small backyard into a farm overnight. One afternoon, he and his close friend Arky came to our home from Ruth and Arky's farm with a pig, a nanny goat and her kid, and some rabbits. Yes, they all went into our back yard! But a few days later our nanny goat jumped our fence and started running through the neighborhood. Dad called Arky to come over and help him catch her. It took them several hours. She was running and jumping fence after fence, yard after yard. Arky and Dad finally believed they had her trapped, but then she started running towards a plate glass bay window, and as she started to jump into the huge window, Dad dove and caught her in mid-air. I thought that was really funny, as was seeing how dirty Arky and Dad were after chasing the nanny goat around all day.

We had problems with our rabbits, too. They weren't getting out; they were getting stolen. One morning when Dewayne and I went out to feed them and clean their cage, they were missing. We couldn't find any place that they could have gotten out, so we were upset and confused. Shortly thereafter, we were walking down our sidewalk and noticed that one of the boys from down the street just happened to have an animal cage with white rabbits that looked just like ours. They had exactly the same markings. We told our dad and he got them back. That wasn't the end, though. Every morning for weeks, our rabbits were mysteriously missing, and they just happened to get into the boy's cage down the street. So, Dewayne and I started sneaking down to his carport and retrieving our rabbits and putting them back in our cage where they belonged. Eventually our dad spoke with his dad, and the rabbits stopped disappearing.

When I was four, I loved to follow Dewayne around all the time even when he didn't want me to, which was most of the time. He and his friend Roy would often go to the drainage tunnels and explore. One day I tried to follow them and suddenly they were nowhere in sight. Because of my ear problems, I couldn't hear them talking in the tunnels. I could only follow by sight. I finally found myself looking at one of the big grates by a street curb where the water drained down into the tunnels. The problem was that I was looking up from below the grate. I couldn't fit through the bars, and I didn't know my way out. I got really scared and started screaming for my brother and for my mom. Mom, Dewayne and Roy heard me screaming and they all arrived at about the same time. Mom tried to comfort me as she sent my brother back into the tunnels to get me. One thing I remember as I think back: my mom didn't ask, "How did you get yourself into this mess?" She just did what it took to get me out.

Sometimes Dad was the one who rescued me. Each day, walking home from school, I greatly feared two Doberman pinchers on a chain that were just down the street from my house. I walked on the opposite side of the street and kept quiet, hoping that they wouldn't notice me. But they always would and they would run full speed at me until they hit the end of their chain. They terrified me. One particular day, the dogs ran at me and the chain broke. I tried to run, but my equilibrium problems caused me to be slow and clumsy, so they caught me and started biting me. The owner ran out and called them off, but then he started accusing me of throwing rocks at them and teasing them. I got home, bloodied, and told my dad what had happened. Dad took me down to talk to the owners, who accused me again. But Dad defended me. He told them he wouldn't call the authorities if they did something about their dogs. It was amazing how nice they became to my dad and me by the end of the altercation, and I never had any more issues with the dogs again.

This is one of those occasions I stood tall when I was walking home beside my dad. I remember thinking, "This is my dad, and I am proud to be his son."

One of the positive things about our family life was our extended family. Where we lived in California, we had a lot of relatives close by, and we always loved going to visit them. We visited our grandparents and great grandparents on my dad's side every week after church. Grandma Suit would tell us to choose what kind of cobbler we wanted, and then she would have all of us kids, including my cousins, go to the garden and orchard to pick our fruit of choice for the cobbler. I can still taste it now!

Spending time playing with our cousins and being with our aunts and uncles was like a family reunion every Sunday. I loved sitting by my Aunt Kay at church. I knew that Aunt Kay loved me, and I would always lay my head against her or sometimes lie down in her lap and sleep. I had peace beside my Aunt Kay, who is very special to me to this day.

Dad's disability income couldn't really support our family, so my mother was always working either at the school or doing other odd jobs to help us out financially. As a result, Carla, Jerry Allen, Dewayne and I were left with our dad for the majority of the time.

Carla was the oldest and took it on herself to try to protect us from dad's anger and abuse. Carla would often take Dewayne and me on wagon rides for fun. I would wait for her to get home from school so that she could take us on a cool adventure. I later learned that this was one of her ways of protecting us from our dad and taking us away from the turmoil of our home.

Whenever Dad punished us, which was all the time, he would make us eat supper in our room. We would beg him to just get the whipping over with, but he would say, "I'll be in there when I'm ready." Most of the time he would wait until bedtime to finally give us our spanking with his leather belt.

Mom tried to protect us, too. She jumped on him more than once when he went after one of us.

One time, Carla brought me extra underwear and even some books to try to protect my behind, but my dad saw what had been done and got even madder, and he got angry at Carla for trying to protect me.

When Dad raged, I would cry for hours, and Dad would get angry at me for crying. I would make paper airplanes with notes on them begging my dad to please forgive me and let me out of my room. He would then whip me for what I had done wrong in the first place, plus whip me for crying and for the airplanes with notes on them. Many times, I didn't know the real reason why I was in trouble in the first place.

Whenever Mom wanted us to stop doing something, and we were refusing to listen, she just had to say, "If you don't stop now, I am going to tell your dad." That's all it took to catch our full attention.

Sadly, for many years, I didn't respect my dad, but I had a deep fear of him because I knew what he was capable of doing. Though I feared him, I deeply desired his love, his attention, and most of all his approval. But I rarely got it.

It has been said that we get our impression of who God is

21

from those we are close to growing up. Especially our father. Dad not only mentally and physically abused us regularly, but always told us that he had a personal relationship with Jesus while treating our family so harshly. How was I going to react to this contradiction? And how would I react when I grew up? Would I react like my dad did and cover up the pain by abusing medications or using alcohol? Would I turn to porn to fill any void that I wanted filled in my life? Would I choose other escapes?

I often asked myself why I would want anything to do with God if my dad was a reflection of who God really is. But even though my image of God took a big hit from my father, God was not without an accurate witness in my life. God showed His true nature through my mother and grandparents, other family members, and also through some great teachers, Sunday school teachers and family friends. Since I saw her every day, my mother in particular gave me a very different view of God. It took me many years of exploration and education to uncover the simple truth that was always right before my eyes.

## CHAPTER 4

# STILL ALIVE

When I was five, we went on vacation to Oklahoma. I loved going on vacations. I didn't love the car ride to get there. Dad and Mom always argued about stopping to get rest or allowing us to use the bathroom. We always carried an old coffee can or a big jar with a lid for us boys to use for our toilet needs so that Dad wouldn't have to stop. Dad never wanted to stop for anything. He had been a truck driver and it seemed like he was always trying to beat his driving time record while we were with him.

The drive to Oklahoma was at least a 24-hour trip. Nonstop. Our discomfort during the trip didn't concern him. He was well medicated. My brothers and sister and I were very uncomfortable from riding, and then we would get aggravated with each other. It was a dangerous thing for us to argue, because Dad was always on edge in the car. On our long journey we drove past the Grand Canyon, Petrified Forest and Meteor Crater, but Dad never stopped at any of them. Mom did her best to keep us occupied so we wouldn't get in trouble with Dad.

After the long, miserable ride, we arrived in Hinton, a small town in west central Oklahoma. We stayed with the Morgans, close family friends from church who had moved to Oklahoma a year before. I loved being there, not only for the fun we all had, but also because it was a refuge from my dad.

After a few days in Hinton we drove to Hugo, Oklahoma to be with my mom's longtime friend, Jaquetta. I have always loved Quetta. She had a farm and, boy, did I love animals. She would have us help milk the cow before breakfast and then she would make us homemade biscuits with some awesome chocolate milk made from fresh cow's milk. I guess it tasted better because we got to help milk the cow.

While at Quetta's, we went swimming at Pat Mayes Lake. I remember being intrigued by my dad's ability to swim out to the buoy even though he had a severe back injury. I was proud of my dad and his many talents even though I lived life in fear of what he might do to us next. Dad was a golden glove boxer and had a gold medal in Jujitsu from his days in the U.S. Navy.

At five years old, I was still almost deaf and I was not supposed to get any water in my ears at all because of my ear condition. As a result, I couldn't swim a lick. (I was unable to go under water until I was 12). We were playing on the lake's beach; not too far away was an inlet with very dark water. I pointed it out to my dad, but he told me not to go over there because it was deep. But curiosity got the best of me and I went straight over there the first chance that I got. I stepped into the water and the next thing I knew, I was looking up at sunlight hitting the top of the water as I sank. When I hit the bottom I tried to propel myself back up, but I couldn't. I finally blacked out.

My dad just happened to be looking over at the inlet and he saw that I was nowhere in sight. He ran and jumped in the water where he saw the bubbles at the surface. Because the water was so dark, he couldn't see me at all. As he dove in he cried out for God's help, and he just started moving his arms in a hugging motion while he was under the water. The water was deep enough that he never touched the bottom. As he was coming back up to the surface for air, he felt me and he squeezed my chest to get the water out of me as he surfaced with me in his arms.

When I woke up, my mother was screaming and my dad was giving me CPR. Quetta said that I looked like a water pump as Dad did chest compressions, with water shooting out of my mouth. After I regained consciousness, I remember my dad taking me back to the beach area where everybody was swimming. He placed me in the shallow water. My mother kept screaming at Dad, telling him to get me out of the water. Dad said to her, "If I don't put him back in the water, he'll be scared of water for the rest of his life." I'm glad he did.

Thank you, God, for saving me, and thank you for giving my dad the ability to swim the way he did that day.

We spent three or four days at Quetta's, and then headed to see Aunt Barbara and Uncle Don near Lake Texoma. They owned a motel, and there was a lot at that motel for my brother Dewayne and I to explore. On our first day there, they were burning trash at the motel dumping area. As soon as we saw the fire burning in the barrel, Dewayne and I quickly found the nearest water hose and put the fire out as fast as we could. We were heroes! Sadly, our dad didn't see it that way and he got mad at us. He was going to punish us for our good deed, but Aunt Barbara and Uncle Don came to our rescue and rewarded us for being heroes.

Later that day I wanted to do something good for them, so I decided to fill up their car for them. My dad always said how expensive gas was, so I saved them some money by filling their tank. With a water hose. Even Aunt Barbara and Uncle Don couldn't rescue me from a spanking for that one.

The next day Barbara and Don took us to Lake Texoma. When I caught my first fish off their cabin boat with a small rod they had bought me, I was so excited! I wished I could have stayed there and fished forever.

Not long after we returned to California, my dad told our family that he believed that God was calling him to be a preacher. I was so excited the day he preached a sermon our church, Shore Acres Baptist. I was thrilled to see my dad up at the podium and sharing God's Word. I had a great hope that this would change the way he treated us at home. In my mind there would be no more yelling at my mother and no more yelling and constantly whipping us, and no more mental head games with us. Mom and Dad even started having Bible studies at our home every week.

One week they were having a Bible study and Dewayne and I were told to go to sleep in Mom and Dad's room. We were playing around in the room and wrestling on Mom and Dad's bed when I got curious and opened a little door to a storage compartment in the headboard of their bed. I found a pistol and I took it out and started playing with it. Dewayne was a little older, and he kept telling me to put it back. I thought it was a toy, but Dewayne knew it wasn't. When I pointed it at him and said, "Bang! Bang!" while trying to pull the trigger, Dewayne screamed out to Mom and Dad. Dad went crazy when he saw me with his gun, and he was going to give me a huge punishment. But Mom stepped in and told him that he should not have had a gun where I could get to it.

I look back and thank God over and over for not allowing that gun to fire. I know without a doubt that God was protecting my brother Dewayne.

Unfortunately, the change I had hoped for in my dad, and we started to see, was only temporary. He kept punishing us. He kept playing head games with us. He would tell us to go to our room, that he was so mad at us that he could beat us to death. Who in their right mind would tell their kids that they are going to beat them to death? He would then make us all of us stay in our room for hours upon hours. Looking back, I can see clearly the effects of medications and alcohol in how he acted toward us.

Soon after this, we actually moved to Oklahoma, where my parents thought we might have a better life. My dad never preached again. He told everyone that he was going to pursue vocational ministry as soon as we moved, but he never did. I don't remember him reading the Bible after we moved, or ever even reading it to me. He continued to go to church every Easter. Our home life stayed in turmoil.

Knowing that we were getting ready to move to Oklahoma, I was saddened because we would be leaving my great grandparents, grandparents, cousins, aunts and uncles, and my best friend David. I would be leaving everybody that I was close to.

CHAPTER 5

# LEARNING THE HARD WAY

I was six when we moved to Oklahoma. We couldn't move into our new house immediately, so we stayed with our friends the Morgans. Less than two weeks after we got there, Mom put me in the Vacation Bible School of the First Baptist Church in Hinton. I was scared and confused. I didn't know anyone there. Change was really hard on me.

We were playing "Red Rover, Red Rover," when it clicked in my head that if I could just break through the barrier of kids that were blocking me, I could keep on running straight to the Morgans' house, which was only two blocks away. All I wanted was to get back to people that I knew and trusted. I broke through the barrier and I ran as fast as I could to their house. I could hear the teachers shouting, "Curtis, please stop! Please come back!" but with all of the fear and confusion built up inside I was determined to keep running as fast as I could. When I finally arrived at the Morgans' home, Joyce Morgan, the mother, was there to meet me. I felt so relieved to see her. She was the only person I had seen all day that I actually knew. I told her that I was running away from VBS. I just knew that

Joyce was going to comfort me and take me in the house, but, boy, was I wrong. Joyce swatted my butt and walked me all the way back to the church.

It was very hard for me to understand why she did this, but now I am grateful, because it taught me to start accepting changes that were taking place in my life, because they were not all bad. I now had to get to know new friends, and VBS was a great setting to do this in. I was so determined to break through the barrier and keep my life the same. The hardest thing for me was getting past what people would think about my difficulty speaking and my balance and hearing issues. I missed my cousin Sue and my Grandma and Papa Brown and my friend David. Why did my whole world have to change because my parents wanted to move to Oklahoma?

I am grateful now because I eventually made great friends and they are still my friends today, over forty years later. We come to know great friends during great challenges in our lives. I have learned that change can be good if it is for the right reasons. God was preparing me from my youth to deal with the many changes in life.

Our new house wasn't as bad as I feared. Actually, it was a blast. The place was an old farm house in Hinton, perfect for a city boy who loved the country.

I adored trees and our yard had several of them. In our front yard was a huge cedar tree, and I had a rope. What a great (i.e., dangerous) combination for me. I thought I was a great climber, but I didn't always think through things completely. (I still have that problem at times today!) I tied one end of the long rope around the bottom of the tree and then I tied the other end to my waist. I began to climb the tree without a care in the world. I just knew that no matter what, the rope would catch me and I couldn't get hurt. I then heard my oldest brother Jerry

Allen calling me and telling me to get down. But I was already almost to the top of the tree. Jerry screamed, "Little brother, what are you doing? You better get down or you're going to fall!"

I responded with confidence, "I'm not worried, the rope will catch me! It's tied around my waist."

He laughed and said, "You need to get down before you fall," but I continued to climb until I got across the highest branch and started down the other side. After I started down the other side, the next branch I stepped on broke, and I went tumbling down head over heels through the branches. Thank God the rope eventually ran out of slack and stopped me just before I hit the last branch.

I did learn from this event in my life. I never tried to climb that way again!

But actually, I learned even more. Looking back at many instances of my life, I realize now that God often used other people to save me from the mistakes I was making. Even when I made bad judgment calls (which was often), God gave me a lifeline to save me.

The tree incident was a good time to learn that sometimes my older brother knew more than I did. I needed to let go of my pride and listen to him. He had my best interest at heart, and it really was God speaking to me through him, wanting to protect me. I have learned through my many bad choices that I need to listen to God and obey His commandments, because He has my best interest at heart.

I can see now that even at the top of the tree God was speaking to me through my brother, and I still had the opportunity to turn back. If I had turned back when I was confronted, I would not have had to experience the fall that I took. It's never too late to turn back, no matter how far we have traveled in the wrong direction. Nor should we allow bad decisions from our pride to determine our outcome in life. Proverbs 16:18 says that pride comes before a fall. In my case it was literally true!

My oldest brother wasn't the only one who tried to rescue me. My mother rescued me many times during my childhood when I was unable to take a stand for myself. Mom stood up for me when I made bad decisions during my teenage years and she even bailed me out as I started having debt problems at a young age. It's amazing to see that sometimes our parents or parent will do anything to prevent an accident or attempt to preserve us from further damage. I have learned that sometimes we need some of those bumps and bruises to teach us a lesson and help us realize that our parents can't always be there to save us. It helps us realize that we need Someone even greater.

I suppose you could say that I rarely learned my lessons right away, though. On another day, I was tying a water hose with a loop to a tree branch in the yard. I was always a daredevil, and this time was no different. To get my foot in the loop, I had to stand on a large drum because the loop was too high to reach. While I was trying to put my foot in the loop, I heard a loud cry from the house. It was Mom. She darted out of the house and explained to me that if the drum fell over and my foot was in the loop, I would be stuck hanging upside down. She said all my blood would run to my head and I could die.

Once again, I had a stern warning, and I chose not to listen. Mom went into the house, and instead of fleeing temptation, I kept looking at the hose and saying, "Self, we can do this." I climbed up on the drum and placed my foot into the loop, and as I started swinging, the inevitable happened. I knocked the drum over. There I was, hanging upside down and crying out, "Mom, come help me!"

After a few minutes, Mom came out and gave me the I-told-you-so speech. She then gave me a push and said, "Why don't you swing on this one for a while and think about what you did?"

She finally came back and got me down and gave me a hug. She said, "I almost lost you once. Please learn a lesson so I don't have to twice."

## CHAPTER 6

# A NEW WORLD WITH OLD PROBLEMS

In Hinton, I woke up in a new world every day. Each morning I would crawl out of bed and I find myself in an old farm house with wheat fields on the south and west sides. Oklahoma was a culture shock, including the accents, which were very different than my California accent. I not only felt the sting of being in a new place with new challenges, but after a few months I also felt the sting of the cold winter air as it hit my face and went straight through my coat and chilled every bone in my body. It seemed as if I couldn't put enough clothes on to keep the cold from cutting through to my skin. Six months later I had to start adjusting to the hot and humid summer.

Adjusting to the 1,800 miles that now lay between us and our relatives and friends continued to be very hard. I felt lonely and empty and broken on the inside. I can't really put into words how bad it hurt me as I tried to accept or deal with the absence of my grandparents and my family that we left behind when we moved to Oklahoma. I know that my parents were trying to make life easier on us, but it did not change the way I felt about the move. I missed my grandma and papa, aunts and uncles and cousins badly, and I still do to this day. I missed my best buddy David. David lived down the street from us and we played together all the time. He didn't make fun of the way I talked, nor did he tease me when I fell from my poor balance or when I wet the bed. He was a true friend.

The longer we were in Hinton, however, the more I adjusted. I remember two things most about the old farm house: it had a cool, old barn and a it had a very dark cellar. When the first bad storm came, we all had to go to down into the dark and musty cellar which, I discovered, was full of slimy, black and yellow salamanders. They were actually friendly and I loved catching them and keeping them as pets. After the storm, my sister Carla went back down into the cellar. Soon I heard a blood-curdling scream from there. I ran to it and saw Carla coming up the stairs, horrified. It was dark and she had stepped on a pitchfork. She was coming up the stairs with it still protruding through her toe. It scared me badly because I hated seeing my sister hurt. I hate seeing anyone hurt. Carla's toe recovered, though she still has the scar.

It seemed as if we were always having major episodes like that. One of the scariest times of my young life came on a warm summer day. My hearing had improved quite a bit by this point. Dewayne was mowing our yard when I heard a loud noise from the mower and then my brother started screaming and grabbing his leg. The mower had run over some wire hidden in the grass and it shot a piece of it into Dewayne's leg. Mom rushed him to the doctor, who took x-rays. The wire had wedged between the two leg bones and it was too dangerous to try to get it out. So, he's lived with it in him ever since.

Someone, of course, had left that wire in the yard, and my

dad had not bothered to check the yard for anything Dewayne might run over. (Dewayne was only eight or so at the time and he wouldn't have known to do that.) We often don't think about how our actions, or lack of actions, will have lasting effects on us or those we love. That wire in Dewayne's leg could still cause him significant problems one day if it migrates too far.

Dad allowed a lot of stuff into our home that damaged us. The physical abuse, of course, was obvious. So was the alcohol and the abuse of pain medications. But there were other things as well. One day I found pornographic magazines by accident that were hidden in our bathroom blanket closet. The images became seared into my memory. Years later, as I was going through puberty, I came across movies on the television that contained the same kind of thing. One night when my grandma and papa were visiting from California, Dad was asleep and Mom was working, and I turned on the TV. On came a pornographic movie that Dad had forgotten to turn off. Dad's activities were uncovered by his own mother and son. Needless to say, it is something I never should have seen.

When I was eight my dad was in the hospital for four months. Mom was pulled in all directions, taking care of all four kids, working, and going back and forth to the hospital to spend time with Dad. I honestly don't know how she did it. In my mind she was a superhero.

Mom got a bit of a break when Grandma Brown flew out from California to help take care of the household and us kids. I was quite a sneaky kid, and by this time I had already developed a chewing tobacco habit. I used to go next door to my buddy Myron's house and indulge. I thought it was cool, but later I experienced how uncool it really was.

One day, Grandma noticed that some of her and Mom's cigarettes were missing out of the freezer on the back porch. She asked me if I knew where the cigarettes were going and, of course, I told her no. The Bible says that we can be sure our sins will find us out. One day I was walking back from Myron's and Grandma stopped me and asked how things were going. I responded with a slurry voice, due to my mouth being full of chewing tobacco.

She said, "Sonny, come up here on this porch with me." I knew I was busted, and I walked very slowly up the front porch steps, fearing I'd be beaten with a belt, since that's what my dad did.

But Grandma surprised me with a unique kind of grace. She said, "Spit for me!" I spit a little way off the porch for her, and she asked me, "Just how good does that chewing tobacco taste?" She then told me that if I am going to chew tobacco, I was going to have to spit a long way.

I spit as far as I could, and Grandma said, "Well, Sonny, you're going to have to spit farther than that to chew this stuff." She told me to try again, and again, and again. I never did spit far enough to chew that tobacco, so she made me spit it out.

She then asked me what I had traded for the chewing tobacco, and I knew that I was busted about the cigarettes as well. She got onto me pretty hard, but her grace and mercy taught me more than a beating could ever teach me. She explained how much those cigarettes cost them and how I was stealing from them to feed my own desires and habit. I was truly sad about what I had done, and Grandma taught me a huge lesson in grace.

Later on in life, I went to visit Grandma after the Persian Gulf War, and I had an addiction to both cigarettes and dipping tobacco. The first words out of her mouth when she saw me dipping tobacco were, "Let's go out in my back yard and see if you can spit far enough to dip that nasty stuff."

I remembered the episode from my childhood, and I said, "Grandma, I will never be old enough to do this in your eyes, nor will I ever spit far enough to prove to you that I am OK to dip it."

She said, "That is just the point I wanted you to see. I love you, and I know what that stuff does to your tongue, lips and throat, and I would never want to see my grandson that I love dearly go through the pain of cancer from something that could have been prevented."

That day, I promised Grandma that I would not dip again, and I didn't, and she encouraged me to quit smoking, and I did, and I also got to see her quit smoking as well. Grandma, thank you for never allowing me to spit far enough. I love and miss you, and I know that this will be an ongoing joke in heaven.

## CHAPTER 7

# MY BUDDY POOCH

In early 1976 I had just been a ring-bearer at my Uncle Johnny and Aunt Helen's wedding in Poteau, Oklahoma. We were on our way home and Mom decided to stop by Aunt Carolyn's house in Stuart, Oklahoma, where Mom was born and had grown up. Aunt Carolyn had a huge farm full of animals and adventures. She had a litter of bird dogs, and I was begging Mom to let me have one, but Mom said that we couldn't afford one. At that point, Aunt Carolyn said to me, "You know, Curt, it is going to be pretty hard to sell that runt there because it's so small. You're the baby of the family, so maybe you could take care of it for me."

I was so excited! Mom said, "I didn't even say yes, yet, Son."

But Aunt Carolyn replied, "There is no excuse for Curt not to have this little puppy, and he is taking him home."

Momma didn't argue with her.

Aunt Carolyn asked me what I wanted to name him, and being a simple person, I said, "How about Pooch?"

She said, "That fits him well. Now, you and Pooch go and play and get acquainted with one another."

Pooch became my best buddy ever! I would run from the house into the woods and climb a tree playing hide and go seek with Pooch. I was a lot faster than he since he was still a little puppy. However, every time I thought that I had hidden from him, he would start barking, and I would look down and he had his nose to the ground until he came to the tree that I was in. He knew my scent and followed it until he caught up to me.

Pooch and I had so much fun together. He was just what I needed when Dad was in the hospital and Mom was always busy. Every time that I got home on the school bus, Pooch was waiting at the end of the driveway for me. He knew just what time to go down there to meet me.

I had Pooch about six months when I had a bad feeling in my stomach on my way home one day from school. I didn't know what was wrong, but I knew something was. I was already heartbroken from all that was going on in our family at the time. Even apart from Dad getting really sick, there was still all the turmoil that had been there for years. Pooch was my buddy and I knew that I could count on him to cheer me up when I was down, running with me through our woods and through the canyon and even sitting down on the horse trails and eating snacks together— all while escaping the reality of what was going on in my life.

I was actually sick to my stomach the whole bus ride home, and when I arrived Pooch was not there to greet me. Jerry Allen and Dewayne shared the bad news with me. When I looked at where Pooch met me daily, I saw that there were tire tracks right where he always sat waiting on me. Our driveway was pretty long and Pooch always sat right inside the entrance, not even close to the road. He had not been hit accidentally. This showed me the cruel reality of some people in the world we live in.

Jerry Allen helped me bury Pooch. That was so hard for me

to do. I was sick to my stomach for days. I felt lost without my dear buddy. Pooch was the only peace that I had at that time, and now the peace was gone forever.

I remember praying to God over and over to please let me wake up each morning and find that God had brought Pooch back to life. I knew He could because He is God, and I knew that Jesus rose from the grave, so why couldn't Pooch? Mom tried to explain that God would help me through this heartbreak and that Pooch was not coming back, but I refused to believe that, and I continued with the hope that he would come back to life.

About a week after Pooch had been killed, our neighbors down the road brought me a dog that Mom let me have, and I named her Goldie. Goldie fell in love with me, and I fell right back in love with her. Little did I know that Goldie and I had something really cool in common. I loved to find tortoises, and so did Goldie. The funny thing is that every time Goldie would find a tortoise, she would bark until I came to get it. My cousin tried to pick one up that she had found, and Goldie jumped up and bit him and kept him away from it until I got there. Goldie also loved to catch wild turkeys, but we never had the chance to see one of those alive once she found it. I had Goldie for about six years, and she was my hunting buddy, my close friend, and my protector.

## Chapter 8

# PLEASE DON'T PULL THE TRIGGER

Life didn't change much for the next several years. Carla left home when I had just started junior high. Jerry Allen left two years later, leaving me, Dewayne, and Mom and Dad. I made Cs in junior high and Bs and Cs through most of high school. I got very involved in athletics, especially football, wrestling, and track.

At home, the abuse continued.

One cold winter night during high school I didn't get the message to stay away from our home. I had been out riding around with some of my buddies downtown and goofing off until my curfew. I went home like I always did and walked through the front door. I could immediately tell that my dad was in a rage, messed up on pain medications and alcohol.

I started to turn around and leave when he yelled at me and told me to stay in the house. I started to leave anyway until I noticed a gun pointing at me. I looked at him with shock and shut the door. Dad came over to me and put the gun to my head. I was terrified. I couldn't believe my own father would do something like this to me. He started ranting about how his best buddy, Lenny, had been killed while tending to my dad's old gas station in Shore Acres, California. Dad kept saying he didn't want to live anymore, and that he was going to take me with him. The whole time Dad was ranting about his buddy, Lenny, I was thinking about not having a future. It looked like I would be dying right there by the hands of my very own father. I begged him over and over, "Dad, please don't pull the trigger!"

With his gun to my head, Dad kept telling me that I would not ever amount to anything (as he often did) and that I could never achieve the things that my oldest brother Jerry had achieved. He reminded me that I was nothing but a punk kid and a ---. Dad kept on ranting about how unfair life is and that he didn't deserve the life that he was handed.

All of my years of life were going through my mind in this short period. I was just wondering when he was going to pull the trigger and get it over with. He hit me with the pistol and then put it back to my head, and by this time, though I was scared, I was actually starting to get angry. I told him to go ahead and pull the trigger because I knew where I was going and it would be much better there than what I had to endure with him during this life. In my heart, I wanted my dad to put the gun down, and deep down, I wanted my dad to just love me.

He lowered the gun.

The next day, my dad was furious and asked my brother Dewayne and I who had hit him. I kept silent and Mom stood up and said that she did and that he needed to leave. Dad packed his bags and went back out to California like he usually did when he and Mom fought.

Sadly, Grandma Brown took up for him over and over. Dad never seemed to have any accountability for his actions towards us. This wasn't the first time that my dad did something like this to one of his children. He always threatened us and beat us. He would stop at nothing to keep complete control over us. In my heart and mind I cried and pleaded to God for peace in our home and for a real family. I often dreamed of having a father like Uncle Don or Uncle Eldred. I wanted so much to tell my wrestling coach, Coach Brack, or my music teacher, Mrs. Chaloner, what went on at our home on a daily basis. Both Coach Brack and Mrs. Chaloner were always there for me, but fear of my dad's retaliation kept me from ever telling them about the physical and mental abuse that me and my siblings endured daily from our dad.

Even though Dad did the things he did to me, I still wanted to have a real relationship with him. If I could change three things in my life, the first would be that this event with the gun would never have happened. The second would be that I would have saved myself and my virginity for the woman that God wanted me to have as my wife. I still remember something my mother always said: "Son, respect women as you respect me and keep your pants zipped until you are married." She also told me many times that I would never regret honoring God.

The third bad choice that I made was when I walked away from my football and track scholarship because of a sexual relationship with a girl many miles away. These choices started a very destructive pattern in my life. I lost my virginity at 17 years old, and, boy, did that put a huge hole in my heart as well as a brokenness in my spirit for many years. The Bible indicates that sexual sin is not just physical, it is also spiritual and mental. My sin started me on a destructive path of sexual addiction.

## CHAPTER 9

# DAD, DO YOU SEE ME NOW?

After many years of seeking my dad's approval, I decided to join the Oklahoma Army National Guard. I was hoping to get my dad to see me as a young man rather than a punk kid. I can see now that many of the things I did in life were to try to capture my father's attention. Sadly, I often simply suffered negative consequences from my attempts, rather than positive reinforcement from my dad.

I signed up for the Oklahoma Army National Guard on March 5, 1985. I was a junior in high school who wanted to get better at sports and get stronger mentally while trying to please my father at the same time. I never knew what kind of hardship the military would eventually put on my life as well as my family. They say hindsight is 20/20, and if I had had the benefit of hindsight at that time, I probably would've made a different choice like joining the air force instead of the army.

I went to basic training at Fort Dix, New Jersey, in May 1985. I was seventeen years old and, boy, did I grow up that summer. Or so I thought. One of the drill sergeants, a Sgt. Brent, challenged me one time, threatening me. I looked him in the eye and told him, "You could never instill the fear in me that my father gave me on a daily basis."

I see now that I was trying to both overcome the fear of my dad as well as trying to please him and gain his approval. Even today, I find myself trying to gain God's approval. But there's nothing I can do to gain it. I can only receive what His Son did for me on the cross.

During my senior year, we were playing Elgin in a huge district football game—the most important game I had ever played in. It was also senior night. The day before, on Halloween, I was literally begging my dad to come and watch me play football for the first time. Dad had never been to any of the sporting events that I played in. He kept telling me he didn't feel well and that it was just too hard on him. I was very broken because I wanted my dad to be there for senior night and to at least see me play one game.

Unfortunately, my pain over Dad not coming to see me wasn't the only thing I had to deal with. Halloween night I was hit by an egg in the eye. I went to see the doctor Friday morning by myself, the day of the game. He said I was lucky I hadn't lost the eye, and he put a patch over it.

Sitting in the exam room, I heard voices coming from the lobby. Students' voices. Teammates of mine were at the doctor's office, asking him to please hurry up because I had to be at school so many hours that day to be able to play.

The time arrived for the game and I kept wondering if by some chance my dad would show up for senior night. My eye was causing me a lot of discomfort as well as some balance issues, and it was rough trying to focus out of one eye. The announcer started calling all of the seniors' names. I couldn't see my dad and I couldn't even see my mother, who was usually there. I was so distraught that I didn't even notice that they had already passed by the letter B. I was tearfully watching all of my senior teammates meet their parents at the fifty-yard line. When they were all out there, the home crowd stood up and cheered. I happened to look down past the west end zone. There, I saw my mom helping my dad out of the car, and then walking with him to the field.

I ran to my dad, crying my eyes out. It didn't matter how many times he had hurt me, my dad was there for me and he came to watch me play. We embraced in the end zone and my mom, dad and I walked together to the fifty-yard line and the crowd cheered as they introduced us. I played the best game of my life with one eye because my dad was there watching me.

Never underestimate the power of a father. Never underestimate the power of God *the* Father in heaven. God is watching us and, as a matter of fact, He is on the field with us.

My senior year saw a lot of accomplishments in sports and academics. I was all district co-defensive player of the year in football. I made the all-senior team in wrestling as well as western conference champion, state qualifier and regional runner-up. I had several scholarship offers for track and football.

I went to McPherson College in Kansas to play football and run track. However, just before college football practices started, I had a sexual relationship with a girl many miles away. I couldn't break away from the sexual and emotional addiction. I thought I had to be with this girl to be happy. I had already made it through two-a-day practices, and I even made the team as a freshman. My college football coach tried to talk me out of leaving, but I was so intertwined with the sexual relationship that I had no ability for rational thinking.

When I went back to the girl, she had nothing to do with me. I had already walked away from my scholarships, and therefore I was even more broken spiritually and mentally. I started reaching out to get any girl I could, with the hope that somebody would love me. If they didn't, I would hurt them as I had been hurt.

I will never forget the first time that I actually heard God's voice. I thought I was crazy when He spoke to my heart so clearly and so loudly that I actually looked around to see where He was or who was speaking to me. I was working at a TIPCO chemical plant near Freeport, Texas, as a helper. I heard God's voice as I was working in the middle of a huge pipe rack that transported the chemicals. I looked all around me, and then I heard it again. God said, "You will preach My Word." When I finally realized that this was really God speaking to me, I looked up and said to Him, "No, God, that's no fun."

What I didn't know at the time was that I was in for a whole lot of no fun, and it had nothing to do with preaching God's Word. Most of it was the result of not listening to God and not obeying His call on my life. In other words, most of the pain would be self-inflicted. I also experienced the pain of feeling like God didn't and couldn't love me because of who I became.

After my encounter with God, I ended up getting in with the wrong crowd and almost went to jail for some crimes that I didn't commit. I was guilty by association. Yes, I did some wrong things, but in my eyes I wasn't as guilty as those I was hanging around with because I did not see myself doing the same things that they had done.

Sadly, I was just as guilty because I chose to be with them and I chose to go the places they went even when I knew it was wrong. One night my friends and I went into a mansion and took some things that didn't belong to us. I had become a follower instead of a leader.

Somehow, my dad came down to bail me out before I even knew I was in trouble. At three o'clock in the morning I recognized his car approaching the beach house I was renting on Surf Side Beach. I was drunk and petrified when I saw him coming. But the first thing Dad said to me when he pulled up was, "Are you going to invite me in and give me a drink?"

I was relieved and shocked and truly happy that my dad was there. This was actually the beginning of our friendship, and it started by him coming hundreds of miles to stand up for his son while knowing his son was in the wrong. I had never experienced this before, my dad stepping in to save me. I had been accused of many things I had not done and he knew that, but at the same time he knew I was guilty and was still willing to do what it took to protect me. I did not know that the others had planned on blaming me for all the wrong things they had done, most of which I didn't even know had happened. I could have gone to prison, but God had other plans. He started building a relationship between my dad and me, as well as putting it on the hearts of the owners of the mansion to have mercy on me.

I started thinking that maybe I wanted to start over and do something worthwhile with my life. I would go on to make many more mistakes, but as I look back, I see God's grace and mercy on my life that were so much greater than the mistakes.

## CHAPTER 10

# AN OCEAN AWAY

After Dad got me out of trouble and I moved back up to Oklahoma from Surf Side, Texas, I thought that I would get back on track. It didn't quite work out that way. I started drinking a lot and hanging around with the wrong crowd and I lost my job. Dad and I stayed away from each other because we seemed to constantly clash. Not only was I a heavy drinker, I was addicted to sex and even sex clubs. Here I was living on a very limited income and spending unlimited amounts of money on booze and strippers. I had grown up in church and I even believed that I had been saved at a young age, but my actions were not even close to that of a Christian.

One night I heard a knock on the door of my rent house. It was my dad. I hesitated to open the door, but he said, "Son, I know you're in there, so open it up." I was a little scared, but I knew it must be important. He entered, looking very angry.

"When are you going to make something of yourself?" he asked.

Then he told me why he had come over. "Your cousin Dianna has passed away from cancer."

It hit me like a ton of bricks. Dianna was only four years older than me. I felt completely broken. I knew I needed to get away from the small town and the crowd that I was hanging with and make a change to accomplish something in my life.

I called an Air Force recruiter the next morning and then took the military entrance exam. I could do anything that I wanted in the Air Force. I needed to get in quickly because I had just been fired from my job. But the Air Force couldn't get me into its school for another three months. I needed a job immediately, so I called the army recruiter and, since I had already completed basic and advanced training, he arranged for me to go straight to Germany with the army. I was leaving on May 15, 1988 for South Carolina and then Germany. My mother was waiting to take me to the MEPS station in Oklahoma City. As we were about to pull away from the house, Dad stood outside, but he didn't come over. I said to Mom, "See, he doesn't love me, because he won't even tell me goodbye."

Mom replied, "You go and tell your daddy goodbye and do it now. He does love you, Son, and you need to let your pride down and be the man you really are deep inside and tell him you love him."

I finally let the pride and fear go and I walked over to him. His back had been to us the whole time, so I quietly walked up beside him.

"I love you, Dad," I said. "I'm sorry for letting myself become the person I am, but I'm doing what I feel is right to make myself a better man."

As my dad turned to look at me, tears were streaming down his face. He embraced me for the first time that I could remember. "Son, I am so proud of you, and I love you very much."

It was the first time that I truly heard my dad say something like that to me. Dad then told me to be careful and follow orders. Man, I did not want to leave my dad's side that day, but I knew that it was time to go, and I had to be in OKC in an hour. I left with a whole different view of my father. I loved that man, and I knew that he loved me in return.

Now I saw why Dad drove all night to meet me at my home on Surf Side Beach at three o'clock in the morning to keep me from going to prison. He fought for me. It was, in a sense, how Jesus left heaven to come down to us and sacrifice His very life to rescue us. As a father now, I see that this is what a true father does. A true father is to be a picture of who our Heavenly Father is.

I was now full of anxiety and some fear because I was leaving for a strange land and would be living with a lot of different kinds of people. But I knew in my heart that my dad was for me in this, and that was all the encouragement I needed.

I will never forget that first night in Bamberg, Germany, where I was stationed. I still had a lot of my bad traits (which I would have for years to come), but God was making His presence known. A great buddy and fellow soldier, Todd Hurley, had gone out to the bars with me and finally we started to walk back to the barracks a few miles away. Strangely, we kept running into similar-looking statues. Todd commented, "Man, there such are a lot of statues that look alike in this country." We walked until daybreak, when we set a bottle on a statue and then resumed walking. Half an hour later we were back at the same statue with the bottle! We had been walking in circles all night.

It's said that the definition of insanity is doing the same thing over and over and expecting a different result. I did this quite a bit while in Germany and even after the war. I believed that God was there, but I wanted to please my desires instead of pleasing God. Mom always prayed that God would place people in our paths that were not ashamed of who God really is and who lived as a reflection of His Son Jesus Christ. God was about to answer her prayer in Germany in the person of Chief SFC Warren.

## CHAPTER 11

# MY SHOCK AND AWE

I grew up in a small Oklahoma town with people of vary-ing races and nationalities. I never really gave much thought to racism because I hadn't been exposed to it. Growing up, I had several black and Hispanic friends that I played with all the time, and I worked with people of different colors at the nursing home throughout high school. My mother was a nurse there for over 25 years. I loved *all* of these people very much and I still do!

While walking in downtown Bamberg, I was jumped by some people of color that were also members of a gang. By the grace of God I got out of it alive. The thing that hurt me the most was that I didn't understand why they were targeting me. In my mind, as an American soldier, I was on their team. I got a concussion and lost some front teeth, as they used a board to rough me up. Chief Warren teases me to this day about how bad I looked after that encounter. I'm so glad I didn't allow it to change how I look at people who don't look like me, because some of my greatest friends have been people of color, and I truly thank God for their friendships to this day.

You could say that if I hadn't been going to the bar that I would never have been beaten up. And that's true. The biggest issue that I was having during my military career was that I just wanted to fit in and be liked. I hadn't trained with the soldiers I was stationed with, but they all knew each other. I was in a strange place, having to adapt to different personalities, while at the same time performing my job as a soldier and mechanic. In addition, every day that I awoke I had to deal with this strange man, SFC Warren, a rough and gruff section chief who reminded me a lot of my dad when I was growing up. You guessed it—I didn't like that a bit.

I was half a world away from everything that I knew, and now I had to grow up. Going out every night and drinking and sleeping around didn't do anything to fill the void in my soul, and it especially didn't help me be a better soldier. I would return to the barracks after a night on the town and with a woman and cry myself to sleep for what I had done. And I would dream of being home.

The sad thing is that I had been doing the very same thing in the good ol' USA, but it was a lot easier to access alcohol and women as a soldier in a foreign country. I would go out nearly every night to the bars and clubs and strip joints and sometimes even where the prostitutes hung out and be with them to try to fill the void. Why was I doing this? I prayed at the time to discover the answer to this, and the first thing that came to mind was that I was trying to find some kind of relationship while trying to escape the reality of being away from home and lonely.

One morning, about 3 a.m., I heard something from the end of the hallway and I went to check it out. The noise was coming from SFC Warren's room. I quietly stood by his door for a few minutes. I realized that he was praying; he even mentioned my name in his prayer.

I immediately thought of my mom telling me that she always prayed for God to put people in our paths who love Him and are not ashamed to share who He really is. I thought to myself, *this can't be happening, because this man is really tough on me and he reminds me of my dad.*

But as I was around him more, whether it was training in Graf or Hoenfels, or in the middle of a blizzard pulling the engine on a howitzer, he was there by my side, or he was bringing me something warm to drink, or a warm HMMV to sit and thaw out in.

As I got closer to SFC Warren, I noticed that the others in my section were starting to dislike him. As I look back, I realize it was because he was an honest, God-fearing man and they obviously feared him. The men even lied about him several times to get command to remove him from Alpha Battery Maintenance team as the section chief. When I stood up for him, a few of them did what they could to make me look bad. The men eventually got me moved to SVC Battery Maintenance so that they would not have to face me, either.

A huge thing that separated SFC Warren from being like my father was that I saw him live out his faith, not just talk about it like my dad did for many years. I also saw SFC Warren truly forgive those who came against him and continue to respect and honor them while always praying for them. He loved them like Jesus Christ loved him, no matter what he had done. Through all of my partying and womanizing, Chief Warren never looked down on me. He even got me to go to church with him several times. Every time I went I was horribly convicted and that made me not want to go. Being addicted to sex and alcohol had become a lifestyle to me, but deep in my heart I could feel God pulling at me no matter how hard I ran, and, boy, did I feel miserable for many years to come. To say nothing of all the bad consequences I suffered. Even as I continued to run from God while in Germany, He kept putting His truth before me daily in the way I saw Chief carry himself through all of the adversity he was walking through. This man whom I despised at first became my best friend. He is still my best friend to this day. Chief loves and continues to pray for those who stood against him. I truly love him like a father.

As I look back on my life, I see many times where God just point blank laid it out to me through another man that I loved dearly, my Uncle Don Robertson. A few years before, Don was by the ocean near San Luis Obispo, CA and God spoke to him as clear as day. He said that the sun was getting ready to set on the water and God said to him: "If you love Me you will keep my commandments." Don's words cut to my heart. You see, I claimed be a Christian and love God. I was even baptized at nine years old. But Jesus to me was just a story in a book. I was claiming these things, but if you really love someone you will be willing to lay your life down for them. I was not even close to giving up my life for God—or should I say my lifestyle. I wanted just enough of God to make me feel comfortable and give me some kind of peace.

The trouble is that it was a false peace. I thought I could go out and sleep with a woman and drink until I passed out and ask for forgiveness the next day and everything was all right. I was lost in lust and perversion and the gods I served were sex, alcohol, and deceit. Those things gave me a sense of escape. But in His grace and mercy, God put Chief Warren in my path. Chief's life kept reminding me of the truth God spoke to Don.

I went home on leave for the first time in April of 1989 after hearing my mother and nephew Jason cry while I was on the phone with them on Easter. Jason asked me to please come home soon, and I couldn't tell him and my mother no. Dad, my cousin Mike and my niece Ashley met me at the airport gate when I came off of the plane and Ashley ran to me and jumped into my arms and wouldn't let me put her down until we got in the car. I miss the days when you could walk your family and friends to the gate and meet them when they came off the plane.

That summer, my dad called while I was serving in Germany. He asked me to come home and see my mother. She was very sick. I had just been home on leave a month and a half before.

I told Dad to contact the Red Cross and have them contact my command and maybe they would allow me to go home. Soon it was all arranged. Several of other soldiers gave me a hard time about going home again so soon. "He just can't take it over here!" they said. I knew that wasn't true. But Mom meant the world to me.

When I got home and saw my mom, I was heartbroken. I had just seen her six weeks before, but now she looked completely different. She didn't look like my mom at all to me. She just cried and said, "I am so glad to have my baby home." I would see her pray at night and she could hardly get down on her knees, but she did. I felt so discouraged about faith because I knew that my mom loved God and she had lived the reality of the gospel since I could remember. Now here she was, dying.

Why would God not heal my mom? My mom loved Him with all of her heart, and as I heard her pray one night it was for me and my siblings and my nephews and nieces, and not even herself. I prayed for my nephew Trent with my mom several times, and I just knew that God was going to heal my mom and Trent. Trent had a severe brain injury due to lack of oxygen as an infant, and he was handicapped for life.

Trent would wake up at around three o'clock in the morning when I was home on leave from Europe and he would kind of yell until I came over to him and sang to him. But God didn't heal him. When Trent died, my brother Jerry was broken over Trent's going home to be with Jesus, and so was his oldest son Tyler. But I know now that Trent is truly healed and rejoicing with his nannie (mom) and papa (dad) and running and playing with all of those who went to heaven before us.

I went back to Germany for my last six months. While I was home for four weeks I attended church, but it was just to get God to do what I wanted, and not for me to change, doing what He wanted me to do. I was horribly broken over my mom's health and Trent's health and the severe brokenness in my family, but I continued to find false peace in sexual relationships and alcohol and everything else. Except surrendering to God. The scary thing is that I started to get comfortable with my lifestyle, and the conviction that I was living wrong was gradually leaving my soul.

When I returned to my base, I had been switched from Alpha Battery Maintenance to SVC Battery Maintenance. I didn't mind. People in my section had been blaming me for mechanical mistakes that I had nothing to do with.

Life at the army base was often stressful and at times tense, but it provided some occasions for belly laughs, too. One time SFC Warren made a bet with Big T that he couldn't beat me in wrestling. Big T was 6'4", weighed 240, and was built like a rock. Big T took the bet and I had no choice but to go along. He kept telling me how he was going to twist me in half. When the time for the match came and SFC Warren said, "Go!", Big T ran at me to bear hug me. I just belly-to-belly splayed him. After I had him on the ground I tied him up with grapevine and he couldn't move at all. He wanted another chance and we went at it again. And I tied him up with grapevine on the ground again. Chief told everyone that he only bet on a sure things. I was glad at least one guy was confident I would win, but it wasn't me!

One cold, snowy night at the Graf training grounds, a couple of the guys went out to go to the latrine at midnight. The wind was blowing so hard it was difficult to hear. But I kept hearing what sounded like shouts. I walked outside the tent toward the nearby wooded area and saw the source of the noise. The two soldiers had climbed up a small tree and were hanging on for life. At the bottom were wild hogs that had chased them up! We finally chased the hogs off, and we laughed about that one for days.

I was supposed to be shipped back to the USA by May 15, 1990, but because we were short on mechanics I wasn't released to go until July 21st, my birthday. I watched Chief and a few of my close buddies leave, which made me sad. I cried out to God for help, but as I look back I only wanted Him to help me with what I felt I needed, not what He wanted me to have.

I continued to use booze and sex as my comforters. Deep down I was looking for something concrete, a real relationship, but my addiction was not just an addiction, it was a war going on deep inside my soul. I truly knew the way to turn, but I kept giving in to the dark side instead of running to the light.

I wish I would have known and applied scripture to my life back then, because I wouldn't have gone through the pain and consequences that I continue to walk through to this day. Just because we know we're forgiven doesn't erase from our minds the mistakes we've made. God allows us to walk through consequences to remind us where we were, how we got there, and where He and only He has brought us to today.

There is a scripture that sums up everything I was doing at that time in my life. James 1:15 says: "Then, after the desire has conceived, it gives birth to sin; and sin, when it is fully grown, gives birth to death." I am truly blessed that I was not dead physically way before this time in my life, especially with all of the sexual diseases that I could have died from. However, I truly was spiritually dead and I didn't even realize it. I was living the reality of this saying: Sin will take you farther than you ever wanted to go, keep you there longer than you ever wanted to stay, and cost you more than you could ever pay. So true!

## CHAPTER 12

# HOME AGAIN! NOT!

On July 21st, my 23rd birthday, I landed at Will Rogers World Airport in Oklahoma City, excited to see my dad and mom. I was now stationed at Fort Sill, only an hour away from them. I loved being able to go see them every weekend if I wanted, and even during the week if I got up very early in the morning.

Dad couldn't pick me up at the airport because Mom was in the hospital, which was disappointing, but some family friends met me. Mom's illness was continuing to progress; it seemed as if every time I saw her she was looking less like the mother I had always known. At the hospital, I felt helpless as I watched her struggle for each and every breath. I just wanted my mother back, but I couldn't do anything to change what was happening to her. When I first saw her at the hospital this time, she grabbed me and hugged me really tight and cried. "My baby came home again!" I just fell to pieces when she did that.

I had gone to Germany and my mom was in great health. When she took her nurse's boards exam she scored second highest in the state. She had gone back to school to become a nurse after working as a Certified Nursing Assistant at a nursing home for twenty years. I was so proud of her and she proved that you can do anything if you set your mind to it. Mom only had an eighth-grade education because she had to help take care of her siblings as she was growing up. She married Dad at sixteen and they stayed married until she went to be with the Lord.

After taking ten days of personal leave, I joined my unit at Fort Sill, Bravo battery 2/18 F.A. The next day, I was introduced to my new motor pool and shown the M110 howitzers, ammo carriers, HMMVs, 5-ton trucks, 2.5-ton trucks and personnel carriers that I would be working on. I would also be driving an M578 (VTR) Vehicle Recovery Vehicle. I was a heavy equipment mechanic for both track and wheel vehicles in a combat unit.

My body was in complete shock due to the heat in Oklahoma. I had been in Germany for almost three years, so my body needed time to acclimate to the weather.

One day I was literally hanging upside down, working on a track ammo carrier M548, sweating profusely. It felt like all the blood was running to my head so I tried to crawl back out of the ammo carrier engine compartment. But I couldn't move my feet. I was stuck. Then I saw that my boots had been tied to some armor bracing. As soon as I realized my predicament, this obnoxious guy named Tommy started laughing his head off.

"Man, would you like some water?" he said. "You look like you're pretty hot. Maybe you shouldn't be hanging upside down so long, because your face is bright red."

He was cracking up the whole time. I looked up at him the best I could and said some things I'm not proud of nowadays, but he just laughed. When one of the other guys approached, Tommy took off. He knew I was furious and he didn't want to be there when someone let me down.

Still angry, I got the ammo carrier running again and headed back to the motor pool office. There was Tommy, standing with his section chief. I gave him a good piece of my mind, and he simply said, "Hey man, do you want to go out and party tonight?"

"Are you crazy, man?" I replied. "After what you just did to me, that's the last thing I want to do."

"Man, it was all in fun. Let's go out and have a good time."

Tommy and I ended up being best buddies. He would come home with me every time I went home. He loved my family dearly and my family loved him back the same way. Tommy would even go up to my parents' house when I wasn't able to go. It made me feel good that he loved my family that much.

(Tommy was also the best artist that I've ever seen. He could bring alive anything with a pencil and a piece of paper. It was amazing to see him draw. On top of that, he was quite the comedian, as I learned early on.)

In the middle of August, after I had been at Fort Sill three weeks, we were called on alert. I figured this was just a training exercise. We had alerts on a regular basis in Germany due to the Cold War and terrorists. But Lt. Col. Rowan called a battery formation and told us that Kuwait had just been invaded by Iraq and that our unit had been put on alert to go over and liberate them. My heart dropped and my stomach cramped. This was the beginning of a nightmare that I wished truly was just a nightmare.

We had virtually no sleep for days as we packed and prepared equipment and loaded vehicles on the train for the Port of Houston, where they would be shipped to Saudi Arabia. Even though I was so close to home, I was unable to go see my parents, but I called them every day. They would tell me what they were seeing on the news and ask me what was going on with our unit. I remember my mom crying so hard and saying, "My baby boy just came home, God. How can you allow him to go to war?" Our colonel finally allowed us to leave the base, but it was on a very strict schedule because we could be called to depart at any time.

Tommy and I went to Mom and Dad's and spent time with my family. Dad tried to talk me into going to Canada and staying with a friend of his so that I wouldn't have to go to war. He said if anything ever happened to me, it would take Mom's life also because she couldn't handle the stress of their baby being in harm's way and possibly being killed.

I didn't go to Canada.

As I look back, I see God constantly working to get and keep my attention focused on Him. During our time preparing for war, I was in church every time the doors opened. Sadly, every time we were allowed to leave base, I was also in the strip joints and bars, partying. I was so confused, but I knew deep in my heart that God was the only one who could save me and protect me. I fought surrendering to Him for many years to come, but I did have a kind of semi-peace through all of this.

God uses everything in our lives to His glory and for His purpose, but I didn't have a clue what He was doing and I was pretty upset with Him. I was upset at Him for not healing my mom. In my heart I knew she was dying. I was upset at Him for not healing Trent, either. I often questioned Him on why He allowed my mom and Trent to get sick. Even though Mom would literally struggle to take her next breath, she continued to trust in God with all her heart, and she never stopped praying or spending time in His Word.

My dad still never went to church or read the Bible, even though we had had one sitting on our coffee table for my whole life. I believe that Mom getting sick and me going to war was God's way of catching my dad's attention also.

Dad and I became very close as the time for me to leave drew near. I would see him praying, which caught my attention, though he didn't know that. Four days before we were scheduled to leave for Saudi Arabia on advanced party, our colonel gave us a weekend pass to go wherever we wanted to go in the USA. My close friend and cousin, Sue, and her husband, Josh, had come to Fort Sill and to Mom and Dad's to see me before I left. Sue and I have been close our whole lives, and always I thank God for her friendship and encouragement. So, Sue and Josh and I went to California to see my papa, grandma, Aunt Kay, Aunt Karen, and Uncle Al.

While there, I went to San Francisco one night to the Haight-Ashbury district to a bar. I got intoxicated and almost got into a big fight with someone who was posing to be a woman and dancing with me. With plenty of foresight, Josh had asked Sue to get the car and meet us out front. He came up to me and said, "Hey, dude, we gotta go now. Sue is waiting in the car out front." That saved my rear—and the person I'd been dancing with as well.

We were going across the Golden Gate Bridge at three o'clock in the morning and I had to go to the restroom really bad. Instead, we pulled over on the bridge and Josh and I relieved ourselves off the side. As if I wasn't making enough bad decisions in life, when I added alcohol they got even more worse. Yet God still loved me after all of this.

The next day Sue took me to the airport. We didn't know if we would ever see each other again, and it was a hard goodbye. When I was called to board the plane, Sue started crying, and I started crying, and she hugged me really tight. I told her that God would take care of me and not to worry, but why would

God take care of a person who would only take Him off of the shelf when he felt he needed Him? But God continued to love me and answer my mother's prayers.

As I was flying back to OKC, I reflected on my life and even started talking to God a little more seriously. I knew in my heart that He was my only hope for survival. You see, it was not just war that God was continually protecting me from; it was from myself as well, and I bet my guardian angels were worn plumb out. I was torn because I had to leave my family. I didn't know if I would see them again, and I wondered if my mom would be alive when I returned.

I landed back in OKC on Sunday afternoon. I was due to be back on post that evening and I was flying out the next morning. I went to Mom and Dad's house. I was standing in their carport, where my brother Dewayne and I built so many things together, and I started crying because I didn't know if I would ever return. I was really scared for the first time in my life, and it was not just for me, it was for my family. As I was standing there in a daze, reflecting on my childhood and wondering about my future, my nephew Jason grabbed my leg really tight, his face filled with tears.

"Uncle Curtis," he cried, "you can't die! God can't let you die! You have to come back home to us!"

I hugged him so tight and started crying even harder, and I told him that God was going to bring me back home.

I didn't really know that to be true, but just as I needed to comfort him, I needed to comfort myself. We went into the house and prayed as a family. I told them not to come see me off the next day, and that I loved them dearly, and I would be safe. Mom and Dad held me so tight that I can still feel them holding me today, and the tears in that room could have filled a bathtub.

I had my brother-in-law Craig drive me to base in my car so that he could bring it back for my folks to use while I was gone. Craig and I shed many tears when he dropped me off at my barracks, knowing that the next day at that time I would be half way to the Middle East, not knowing if I would be coming back.

So here I was, trying to depend on God, and that night I went to the bar with several of my buddies, including Tommy, and I put Him back on the shelf again for that night. I had a pattern of escaping reality with alcohol, sex and cigarettes, and the reality was that these things always caused me harm in the end. We got back to base in time to get our uniforms on and go to the bus with our unit, and, man, was that a heartbreaking sight as all the family members of the soldiers were there weeping and crying as we loaded up and left. I will never forget that sight, and I'm so glad I didn't allow my family to come because it would have really broken me, and I can't imagine what it would have done to my mom. The nightmare just seemed to continue to get deeper, and wild women and alcohol didn't cover up the fear and the brokenness.

## CHAPTER 13

# MONTHS IN HELL

The flight to Saudi Arabia, including layovers and delays, lasted 23 hours. I tried to sleep on the way over, but the anxiety on the plane was unreal. I had been stationed with these men for a month at most and now I had to depend on them, even putting my life in their hands. They were probably thinking the same about me.

We landed in the middle of the night at Dhahran airport in Saudi Arabia. I stepped off the 747 and was stunned by my first breath of air. How could any place be so hot? We were taken to a Saudi national guard unit barracks until daylight. Tommy and I went looking for a bathroom and, seeing a button on the floor, Tommy said, "I wonder what this is?" and pressed it. He found out what it was. The next thing Tommy knew, he was shot in the face with a stream of water from the bidet. Neither of us had ever seen one before.

That night was the last time we got to use a bidet—or even a real toilet—for months to come. By noon that day we had moved to near the Kuwait border to set up our position. My job, I knew, was vital to the operation. Being a mechanic, I had to keep the equipment battle-ready at all times. Tension was thick in the camp; everyone was nervous, and the heat was unbearable. It could reach up to 130 degrees and if you weren't covered up, you would burn almost instantly. The guys argued frequently and even fought at times. I could tell that we simply had to pull it together in order to function as a war machine against the enemy, and not against ourselves.

We slept out in the open the first few nights. After seeing scorpions and snakes during the day, I made sure my feet were inside a sleeping bag. Late the first night I felt something crawling around my feet. I froze and started praying, asking God to please not let it be a snake or a scorpion. After several minutes, I looked toward my feet and saw a kangaroo rat come out of my sleeping bag. I almost lost it, and then I just wanted to laugh. The next day we all started catching scorpions to bet on scorpion fights. Food, especially beef jerky, and cigarettes were the stakes.

We were issued Saudi desert tents. We set up on each side of our maintenance truck and parts trailer, with a huge desert camo net covering our entire position to avoid being identified by Russian satellite. We had a couple of little kangaroo rats that we could feed by hand, and they would visit us at the same time every evening. This was our entertainment, until one day I went to pick up my laundry bag and the bottom had been chewed through and the snacks that I kept in it had been either eaten or torn into. I grabbed a shovel and went after the rats. My friend Bob started laughing and got in my way, protecting them. He thought that was really funny, until they did the same to his bag and food. After that we both went after them with shovels.

After a month or so the guys' trust in one another had grown. Being one of the main mechanics, I was always busy working on our equipment. James (Wolf) was my right-hand man, always working by my side. Wolf and I were both country boys, and country boys can survive. I worked as well with PFC Jeff, a hard-working mechanic and a country boy as well.

Trouble in our unit came from Sgt M, a little guy with a huge inferiority complex. He was scared and on edge all the time and had it out for just about everyone except SFC W and me. Sgt. M and PFC Jeff clashed frequently.

One day Sgt. M pushed him too far and the next thing I knew, Jeff had the end of his M16 barrel in Sgt. M's chest and was about to pull the trigger. Sgt. M wasn't smart enough to try to talk him down. He kept putting Jeff down as usual. I don't know why he thought ordering Jeff around some more would keep him from pulling the trigger. I could see Jeff getting more and more tense, and his finger was getting heavier with every word that Sgt. M said.

Finally, I looked over at Sgt. M and said, "Would you just shut up before you're carried off in a body bag, you dummy?" You wouldn't believe the look he gave me.

I had built a little trust with Jeff because we had worked on equipment together in the USA and I had befriended him. I could see that he was ready to pull the trigger and I had to do something quick. I said, "Jeff, is it worth wasting a good bullet that you may need for the enemy on this guy? Heck man, we need every bullet that we can get out here, and you sure don't need to waste it on him."

Jeff looked over at me, and that was my chance. I grabbed the rifle barrel and put it to my chest and said, "So now, are you going to shoot me?"

Jeff looked at me and said, "Heck no, you're my buddy, and man, you're flat-out crazy!"

I got the rifle away from him, and Sgt. M started running

his mouth again and threatening to punish Jeff. I told him, "It's best that you leave Jeff alone and start treating him like the man he is. Let go of your ego before you're carried home in a body bag before the ground war."

The days turned into months. We were just ready to get this war over with, all the while hoping for a peaceful solution. We were all trusting each other more and getting along better (except for Sgt M), but I was having to work a ridiculous number of hours. The sand and heat exacted a terrible toll on our equipment.

One day I ate an MRE (ready to eat meal) and I got so miserably sick that I thought that I was going to fall out, but I had too many howitzers to get and/or keep battle ready, and we knew that the ground war could start anytime. I had to go to Doc and tell him that I kept losing everything that I tried to eat, and I found out that I had a bad case of food poisoning and that I was severely dehydrated. Doc had to put a couple of IV's in me, we taped the saline solution bags to my Kevlar helmet, and I continued to work on the equipment while getting re-hydrated.

Our unit was chosen to guard an ammo storage in southern Saudi, and we were going to get a few breaks while doing so. I couldn't wait for a little rest. We drove for hours to get to the ammo storage, and just as I had set up my cot and unpacked my duffel bag to rest, Major Warner, our Battalion XO, came up to me and said, "SPC Brown, we're planning a movement to the border of Iraq and we need our equipment ready to go as soon as everybody gets back from this duty."

I said, "Well, sir, can I just get one good night's rest?"

He shook his head. "I'd love for both of us to, but we have to get back up north ASAP." He then told me that we would stop and rest at Dhahran and I could use the phone to call home.

I had been in Saudi Arabia for four months and I hadn't yet called home once.

After we left Dhahran, we drove through the hot, hot desert to our battalion position near the Kuwait border. I met SFC W and Sgt M at the maintenance tent. Tommy, Jeff, my sidekick Wolf, and the rest of the unit were still at the ammo storage. I'd been looking forward to a break from working on equipment. And from Sgt M. As it was, I just had to make the best of it.

We all knew that Sgt M was very timid and that you could scare him easily. Our warrant officer told Sgt M to bring him the parts out of the box behind the driver's seat in an HMVV. As Sgt M walked off, the warrant officer told the rest of us to watch closely. When Sgt M opened the box, he fell to his rear and started crab walking across the sand as fast as he could. I walked over to see what he was trying to get away from. It was huge prehistoric-looking lizard. When I say huge, I mean about three feet long plus the tail and big around. The lizard was following Sgt M as he crab walked. He was yelling at us and telling us to grab that thing. We were all howling.

That evening we saw a dark cloud coming over the horizon. It was the first dust storm I had encountered. We ran ropes from tent to tent, to the HMVVs, and to the shower and bathroom. I was glad our tents were so thick because the sand was horrific. When you stepped out of the tent you had to use the ropes to guide you because you couldn't see anything at all. The next morning we had to clean out every air filter and clean off all the equipment, a very long task.

Our unit finally finished guarding the ammo storage and all the guys came back. I was glad to see Wolf, Tommy, and Jeff, and it was good to have Jeff and Wolf's help working on the equipment again.

SFC W approached me a few weeks later. "Brown, would

you like a break for a day?" he asked.

"Of course. What's the catch?"

"You need to drive the five-ton with several of the guys over to Brigade (about an hour away)."

"What's going on there that's so special?"

"Vice President Quayle will be there and they're having a meal." I thought, *If the vice president is there, the food has got to be really good. I'm all in.* By the time we arrived at Brigade we were all covered with sand from the drive. We went to the tent and there was a line leading to the vice president. I stood in line and waited my turn to speak to Vice President Quayle and shake his hand. When I was next in line, the guy in front of me, from my unit, was shaking his hand and wouldn't let go. He kept asking the vice president when he could go home to see his family. The secret service men edged a little closer to him. I leaned over to one of them and said, "We have been out here for over five months. This guy has a wife and children that he misses and he doesn't even know if or when he's going home. He's unarmed, by the way." They very politely escorted him to the food line.

I stepped up to Vice President Quayle and shook his hand and told him that I only had one question.

"Go ahead," he said. "Shoot."

"Can you spell *potato* yet?"

We both had a good laugh and then I went to eat some good grub. The laugh was on me, though. The good grub was actually cheese sandwiches and chips. Can you say disappointed?

CHAPTER 14

# PREPARING FOR BATTLE

It was a hot December day when our unit and some Marines went up to the berms. (Berms were huge sand mounds that the Iraqis had built on the Saudi border for defense.) We were seeing how the Iraqi Republican Guard would respond to us.

During this drill I was supposed to be an injured soldier, so I was lying on a cot when Tommy was told to put an IV in me. He knew how I hate needles. After he had the needle in my vein, he touched the IV sleeve and said with a huge grin on his face, "Oh shoot, it's contaminated now." I could have shot him for that. He then started another IV and did it right this time, but he laughed at his own joke for an hour.

While the training exercise was going on, Tommy's howitzer caught on fire. The M109 Howitzer weighs 63,500 pounds and its gun barrel shoots two hundred pound rounds for miles. This one was loaded with rounds and black powder bags. The whole thing blew up, sending the huge barrel about fifty feet through the air. The armor nearly all melted to the ground.

As Tommy was running from it, a piece of shrapnel stuck in his Kevlar helmet. But Tommy wasn't hurt and neither was anyone else. After the fire died down, the section chief went over to see if anything could be salvaged. Unfortunately, all of the clothing and food that belonged to the crew had been completely destroyed. However, one miraculous thing had taken place besides Tommy not being injured. The section chief found his Bible in the middle of the melted-down armored gun. Only its edges had been burned, with no damage to the rest of it at all. I thought, *Wow! I will never forget this as long as I live!*

I had been attending Bible studies regularly while I was in Saudi Arabia, and I had even been reading my Bible regularly for the first time. I couldn't understand most of it, but I kept reading it. I knew in my heart that the answers to life were in this book and I believed that it was God's Word. My Bible went everywhere that I went. It had even gone to Europe. A dear Sunday school teacher I had as a young boy, Dixie Snow, gave me this Bible in 1975, and I still have it to this day. I had several people comment to me that I seemed to be at peace no matter the situation, but inside, there was an ongoing battle in my spirit.

We returned from our exercise at the berms and set up our position near the Kuwait border once again. That night we had army-style professional wrestling. The maintenance team was challenging Tommy's section that night. Wolf, who was a big ol' boy, told me I had more moves than Ex-lax, because I could always tie him in a knot. The friendly battle went haywire when Tommy came in from guard duty to an unexpected wrestling match. A guy named Wilson jumped Tommy from behind and slammed him to the ground. Tommy literally thought he was being jumped—not the first time something like this had happened over there.

Tommy went ballistic on him. He grabbed a shovel, not

knowing what was going on. Nobody could talk Tommy down except me. I said, "Please don't hit him with the shovel," and I told Wilson to please shut his big mouth because he kept smarting off.

Tommy put down the shovel and we walked together over to his tent and sat down and talked.

He saw that he had received another care package from Dixie Snow, my old Sunday school teacher. Tommy told me that she had been sending him packages regularly, with food and treats and small cartoons that talked about God and Jesus. He said, "I understand why your mom and dad and family send me stuff, but this lady doesn't even know me."

I said, "She loves you because she loves Jesus." Then I got up. "Wait a minute and I'll be right back." I ran over to my tent and got my Bible that Dixie had given me in 1975. I showed it to Tommy. "Here, read who gave this to me."

"Wow," he said, "this is the same lady that is sending me care packages and those interesting cartoons."

"Yep." She was loving him just as she had loved me.

The next day seemed like it lasted several days. We had a scud missile alert due to the Iraqis firing scud missiles at Israel. We knew that they were very capable of firing them at our position also, since we were attached to 1st Calvary. We had to stay in fox holes for hours and hours in the heat while staying alert in case one came out of the sky. But none came, and fortunately Israel didn't retaliate. If they had, all the Arab nations around us, including Saudi Arabia, would have attacked Israel.

We were still set up on the Iraq border when the air war began. We watched the fighter planes and bombers fly over us for weeks, heading to bomb Baghdad. It was nearing the time that we had dreaded: the ground war.

I just prayed and longed to get it over with. We were ready

for this war—ready to do what it took to win and win fast. Colonel Star told us that we would take no prisoners. A few nights before we finally crossed into Iraq, we had a Nuclear/ Biological/Chemical alarm go off and we all had to get into MOP level 4, which meant that we had to put all of our chemical gear on. At the same time, we had a heat-seeking missile hit our generator, which caused several people to go crazy. You find out who is really ready, and it seemed like the people that acted like they were the toughest were the ones who were scared the most.

Wilson ran over to where I was, the foxhole I had dug. He kept saying, "I'll never get to see my new baby or my two-year-old son and wife again." He hadn't dug a foxhole for himself, so I told him to take my fox hole.

"Why are you giving me your foxhole?"

"Because my family and I both know where I will be if I'm killed, in heaven with God. My mom and dad will be cared for fine if something happens to me."

I was lying in the prone position next to the fox hole, and Wilson looked at me as if I was crazy. "You know," I said, "if God wants to take my life, He'll do it with me in the foxhole just as well as me lying here."

Wilson started asking me about God, and I was more than willing to share. I can see now that God was working on my life even when I was running from Him as fast as possible.

The next night was the night before we actually went into Iraq. I will never forget that night, because God made Himself more real than I had ever experienced before. I was sitting in a fuel tanker with a buddy, David. The tanker's windows were up, and we had just received our last mail call for quite a while. I saw a letter from my dad. I was surprised because Dad never wrote letters. I was in tears when I saw that he had written me, and what perfect timing it was, the night before we went into Iraq.

In the letter, Dad said that he prayed for God to surround me with His angels and protect me. Next, he wrote that God gave him a vision and that Clon Daddy (my great grandfather whom we all loved dearly, who passed away in 1978) could feel the wind from their wings as they went to protect me. The moment I read this, a huge breeze came through the fuel tanker. David looked up from reading his mail and asked, "Where did that breeze come from? The windows are up." Though I had many questions about God, I knew that He sent that breeze, and He made it clear that He was watching over me.

*CHAPTER 15*

# THE GROUND WAR

The ground war began. We opened fire with all the howitzers in our battalion. Could you ever feel the adrenaline as
those two-hundred-pound rounds roared out of the barrels and
flew over into this god-forsaken land called Iraq. It seemed we
moved across the berms as fast as the rounds left their tubes.
After months of preparation, we were motivated and ready to
get the job done. All I could feel was pride and the willingness
to do what it took to free the Kuwait people who had been tak-
en captive and raped, murdered and beaten daily for months. I
was even willing to lay my life down for them.

I rode in the back of the maintenance truck for several miles
as we were raced towards Kuwait, until we hit a rut and lost
our parts trailer. We stopped for a second to grab the things
that we needed most. Before we had even stopped, my buddy
Bob jumped out of the truck and ran to the trailer while it was
moving because his snuff was in there. Man, what a person will
do to satisfy their addiction. Addiction will do strange things
to you, leading you to make irrational decisions that you would
never have made prior to the addiction.

After traveling several miles with the howitzers moving at top speed, we had a howitzer throw a track and break a road wheel. We were told that the unit must move forward and stay with 1st Calvary, so Major Warner asked me to stay behind with him and the gun crew to get the big gun rolling again. Trying to fix this track in the sand was one tough task, and I had to short track it because the rear road wheel arm had broken and so had the torsion bar that gave it tension.

We watched as our unit drove away and the dust settled. Then we started seeing more dust from another direction on the horizon. The roaring engines started getting louder and closer. And we realized that these were not our tanks.

The noise came from T72 Russian-made tanks that the Iraqi army was using, and they were headed our way. I told the gun chief to turn the power off and manually turn the turret in the direction of the tanks. "Put a DPICM round in," I told him. DPICMs deployed several land mines when they exploded. I looked at Major Warner and said I would go out like Rambo and not be taken prisoner. Major Warner was looking at the Slug-go (an old military term for GPS) to see if he could find out our exact position and call it in. But with those old GPS units, you had to wait for a satellite to go over before you could get a signal. There wasn't a satellite over us at the time.

I was working as hard and fast as I could to get the track back on after getting the broken road wheel and road wheel arm off and out of the way. The crew was standing guard and ready for anything, and those that weren't were helping me. You talk about nervous; I saw men praying who normally didn't believe in God. I finally got the howitzer going, and about the same time Major Warner got a signal and called it in, and Apache helicopters took out the Iraqi tanks.

As I look back on Slug-go incident, I am reminded about

how scripture tells us to wait on God. If we had undertaken on our own to move out without knowing where we were, we could have headed directly into the enemy without knowing it. Psalm 46:10 says, "Be still, and know that I am God; I will be exalted among the nations, I will be exalted in the earth."

Major Warner and I were on police action for the rest of the war, and we actually worked together much longer than that. We got the big gun back to our unit, and then we had to go find lost soldiers and broken-down equipment on our own. We came across Cof-Dog (Coffey), whose ammo carrier, full of black powder bags and two hundred pound rounds, was broken down in a minefield. Wrong place, wrong time. Thank God nothing had blown up except a HMVV tire.

"Hey bro," he said, "I'm starving. I haven't eaten in days."

"You hold on just one minute," I said. I went back to Major Warner's HMVV and shared a huge can of sardines that Mom and Dad had sent me. Then we got his tracked ammo carrier running again. Cof-Dog became a close friend with me and my whole family. He would often stay at my mom and dad's house with me and go to the lake with me to see my sister and her in-laws and friends. He was family just like Tommy. So was Wolf and his family. Cof-Dog always told everybody that I saved his life by getting him out of a minefield. I never looked at it like that. I was just doing my job to get my brother back to our unit and in a safer environment.

We arrived at an abandoned Iraqi position late one night. Mines were all over the place, so we had to watch every step we took because it was literally zero alum out. All we had were our red lenses on our flash lights, and we had to be careful not to be seen by the enemy. But none were nearby. Wild dogs ran around everywhere. They were really crazy because they had been feeding on human remains. So had the huge buzzards.

## CHAPTER 16

# THE DAY MY WORLD STOPPED

On March 1, four days after the ground war began, a cease fire was called. Over 100,000 Iraqi soldiers had been killed and over 300,000 wounded. We had lost fewer than 300.

We were set up in an old Iraqi position that 1st Calvary had taken out. We were so relieved and excited about the possibility of finally going home. I was about to pull Tommy's howitzer engine to replace an oil line when he approached and asked me to join him in checking out the bunkers and make sure that there were no Iraqi soldiers hiding out in them. We knew they would still kill us, probably not having even heard of the cease fire. I stopped working on the howitzer. I wasn't going to let my best buddy go out there without me by his side.

As I was getting my army gear back on, a helicopter landed with the parts that we had been waiting on for the repair work. SFC W looked over at me and said, "We need to get the howitzer running ASAP in case the cease fire is lifted and we have to move out again."

Tommy said to me, "Don't worry, brother, I got this," and he got Sgt C to go with him.

"Be careful," I told him as they walked off.

Less than a minute later, I heard a loud boom and my heart fell to the ground. It was like God spoke directly to me and said, "Pray now that his last thoughts are of Me." I did just that as I started to run toward Tommy. But SFC W and someone else tackled me and kept me from going to him. Tommy had been blown up by a mine. He was killed instantly. Sgt C had been hit by the shrapnel too, but he survived and was flown to the nearest navy hospital ship.

Could this be real? Did this really happen? Why God? Why?!

Wolf and Bob ran over to Tommy and tried to save him, but it was hopeless. They got Sgt C ready to fly out to the medical ship. Wolf, Tommy, Bob and I were really close friends before the war. Wolf and I are like brothers to this day.

We had a memorial service right there at the Iraqi position that we were set up in. I can still see Tommy's boots, rifle and Kevlar helmet standing there alone. As we loaded up and started to move out, my heart was so broken. It seemed like I was just dreaming. I was leaving my best buddy behind and there was nothing I could do about it.

That night, I thought that I was dreaming, but I know that I was awake. It was as if God was saying, "Tommy is with me," and that was my biggest concern. I had been such a bad influence for so long, and I was hoping that somehow Tommy came to know Jesus as his Savior. I had a vision of Tommy ascending into the clouds and he looked down at me with a smile on his face and said, "I am OK, brother, and thank you." After that, the vision went away, and it was as if God said to me once again that Tommy was with Him in heaven.

I see now that God was working on my heart and I was starting to listen. God knew that I would as long as I was at war. He has to allow us to go through trials and tribulations to teach us who He really is and to keep our attention on Him. I was very upset at God for allowing my best buddy to die, but I also knew that God was my only hope in life. As a soldier, I understood surrender, but fully surrendering to God was not on my agenda, nor did it make sense to me at the time. Surrender was a bad word to me. I had been taught by my dad and my military training to never give up and to never surrender to anything.

I kept holding on to the battle, and I lived on the battlefield for many years after I went home. I blamed myself for Tommy's death, telling myself that if I had just gone out with him he would still be alive. I felt it should have been me instead of him who died out there.

But the 100-hour war was over. I was exhausted and completely on edge due to Tommy's death. I had had no sleep at all during that time. We were moving our equipment back to a staging area in south central Iraq when we saw a child and his mother in the middle of the desert. Saddam Hussein had made people fight who weren't soldiers; if they refused he either put their family members in the middle of the battle zone or killed them. These two were literally starving and dying of thirst. I gave them the last MRE's I had for myself and some water and told them to watch for the convoy coming, which would help them. A guy told me I was crazy for giving up my food and water.

"I can get more," I told him. "They can't."

From the staging area almost everybody was transported down to Khobar Towers to prepare to go home. We had been over there for almost nine months. I was assigned to stay with Major Warner and ensure all of the equipment was transported and loaded on ships at the Port of Jabal in Saudi Arabia. Major Warner and I had become close friends. I trusted this man like no other while I was over there, and he trusted me the same.

We got the equipment to another staging area near the port, where it had to be fixed and cleaned before being shipped back to the USA. Major Warner told me that Charlie Battery had a track vehicle that needed the engine pulled and a new oil line put on. I couldn't believe it. The mechanics in southern Iraq knew this needed to be done before it had ever been loaded on a truck and driven to the port.

The crew and Charlie Battery mechanics were already flying back to the USA. I was overwhelmed with all of the battalion equipment I had to deal with, and now here was another job that already should have been done. I told Sgt Y that I wasn't going to pull the engine and replace the oil line. "Have the mechanics from Khobar Towers do their job before they fly out."

Major Warner heard about it. "I understand your frustration, Curtis, but you need to do this."

I shook my head. "No. I'm not doing it."

The guys standing there were shocked that I said that to a high-ranking officer. Major Warner told me to go pack my bags. I was going to be shipped down to Khobar Towers and flown back to the USA. So, I went to the tents and started packing my bags. A few minutes later, Major Warner came in the tents and asked somebody to give him some coveralls to wear.

"What are you doing?" I asked him.

"I'm going to help you fix this vehicle. You're going to finish the job you were assigned, and I'm going to do whatever it takes to help you get it done."

This time I was shocked. He worked right by my side the whole time. I looked up to him even more after that.

At the Port of Jabal I slept near the water right by the ships so that I could make sure that the equipment was running and that it was loaded on the ships safely and properly. Major Warner stayed in the nice officer quarters, of course, and was driving a Toyota SUV. And I became even more thankful for him for what he did for me and others. He would come stay out on the port so I could use his Toyota to take other soldiers to the airport and use the phones to call home. And every day he would take me to his quarters to eat good food and to shower and shave.

It was almost time for my ship to leave for the USA. The trip to the Port of Houston would take a month. I was actually looking forward to being on the ship and simply resting. Major Warner and I had gone to the airport to call home. I told my mom and dad that my ship would be leaving in a few days and it would be about a month and a half before I'd be home. Mom started crying. She was worried something might happen to the ship. She tried to catch her breath, but then she started crying even harder.

Mom finally was able to say, "We thought we lost you when Tommy was killed because for days they wouldn't give out the name of the other soldier. We just knew it was you with him because you guys never left each other's side." Then she started crying again. "I can't lose you, Son! I can't lose you!"

Dad was trying to calm her down. "It's OK. He's just doing his duty."

Major Warner was talking on the phone beside me, but he kept looking over. He asked for the phone and started talking to my mom and dad. He said, "Mrs. Brown, your son will be home in a couple of days, you have my word."

I interrupted while he was on the phone. "Sir, what do you mean? I have to take the ship home."

He told Mom and Dad that he was giving me his airplane seat and that I would be catching the plane out of Dhahran the next afternoon. I was stunned. I started getting very excited about seeing Mom and Dad. After Major Warner and I got back to the port that night, he said he had something for me. He handed me a Coin of Excellence medal and said, "This is from Colonel Star and me. Thank you for being a great soldier and a great person. I'll never forget the time that we served together."

I was speechless.

I pray that you read this someday, Major Warner, because I think of you often. I was so blessed to serve by your side.

## CHAPTER 17

# THE MIND WAR STARTS

I landed at Altus AFB and as I was getting off the 747, the commander of Fort Sill, General Miller, met me at the door of the plane as I stepped out onto the stairs. I immediately started setting my gear down and went to salute him. But he put out his right hand and said, "SPC Brown, welcome home. Job well done."

Looking back, I realize that these are the exact words I want to hear from Jesus Christ when I arrive in heaven. And there's a correlation between my highest commander meeting me as soon as I stepped back onto American soil to congratulate me and tell me job well done—there's a correlation, I believe, between that and us being welcomed to heaven.

We are all in a battle. This life is a battle and we are constantly walking on a spiritual battlefield. Where we are spiritually reveals itself through our thought patterns and our actions. I was programmed to be a fighting machine and I did what it took to survive in the physical war. I also knew what I needed to do to survive the spiritual war (at least some of what I needed to do), but at this point I was losing that war.

I got to Fort Sill and we all walked into the huge hanger where we were surrounded by a large crowd of people welcoming us home. I looked and looked for my family and then I saw Mom in her wheel chair and Dad standing behind her, both with tears streaming down their faces. My nephew and nieces ran out to greet me. What a thrilling time that was!

As I hugged and kissed my family, I actually forgot about the war for a minute, and what had happened there. My nephew Tyler asked to wear my desert hat. I said, "Buddy, it's part of my uniform and I have to keep it on."

General Miller was there and overheard me. He said, "SPC Brown, let that boy wear that hat and stand tall."

I can't explain the feeling I had then. It was like dream that I never wanted to wake up from. My mother's and father's and family's prayers had been answered and I came home safe.

My mom and dad drove me to my barracks. I put my things back in the same room I had been away from for months. The three of us and the whole family then went to Pizza Hut. Boy, was that a mistake. I had been eating T-rations and MRE's for months. The pizza tasted great and I ate plenty of it, but was I miserable afterwards! I went home with Mom and Dad, came back a few days later to the base, and then signed out on thirty days' leave. I would soon learn firsthand what a fellow soldier and friend had told me the day I returned. SFC K was a Vietnam veteran who served two tours there. He taught me a lot about survival during war. When we got back, he said to me, "Brown, remember this: now that the war is over the battle of the mind begins."

Unfortunately, I started making decisions immediately that ensured I would lose the mind battle, and the spiritual one as well. I knew that God had parted the Red Sea for me and saved me from disaster, but I went right back to my old ways and the same old crowd. After signing out on leave I headed straight to the strip joint and got drunk and smoked my cigarettes. Once again, I hooked up with a woman and I fed my fleshly desires. I kept saying *no* to God, yet He kept loving me.

I caught a plane the next day and flew to California to see my cousin Sue and her husband, Josh. Most of my dad's family still lived in California as well. I'll never forget watching Sue look for me after I had deplaned. I walked up to her and said hello and, boy, was she shocked. I guess the desert sun had made me pretty dark and I had dyed my hair blonde on top of that.

What a wonderful feeling it was to see my best friend and cousin and her hubby and my Aunt Bo. A few days later we went up to Aunt Barbara and Uncle Don's home in Orville. They had a big get-together for me with a lot of family I hadn't seen in years. Sue got very sick, though, which scared me badly. Thank God her close friend Katy, about to graduate from nursing school, was there to help her. The battle in my mind started hitting me when Katy and I and some of her friends went to a club near Chico College. I had several drinks and then it hit. The crowd kept growing bigger and bigger and the music kept getting louder and louder and I felt like the whole world was closing in on me. I couldn't control my emotions, and I was getting scared and angry at the same time.

Katy took me back to the apartment and her roommate's mother was there. The mother sat and talked with me for a very long time until I finally was able to go to sleep.

I finally went back down to the Bay Area to see my grandparents, aunts, uncles, and cousins from my dad's side of the family. I woke up one morning at Papa and Grandma's house and I was confused. I didn't realize at first where I was. I got very anxious and angry and I was looking for Tommy. In my brokenness and fright, I finally got down on the floor in the prone position, hoping all of it would just go away. I felt a hand on my shoulder and I heard a calm voice. "I love you, Sonny. I know that God loves you and He is right here with us." I started crying so hard because I wanted to believe that, but I felt that God had deserted me because I had walked away from Him. Papa hugged me tight and began to pray and just hold me until I finally calmed down. Papa, I love you and I miss you and I am so grateful for having you as my papa.

The next day I went back to Sue's house in Rodeo. I was waiting for her to get home from teaching, and when she arrived she tried to sneak up on me and goose me. The war kicked back in and my immediate impulse was to level her. Thank God I didn't. But I scared her—and myself—with my response. The next day I got a big laugh out of her by having a shovel in my hands in the back yard and acting as if I was digging a hole.

Sue asked, "What are you doing with that shovel?"

I said, "Rumble (their dog) and I were just using the bathroom and I had to dig a hole for mine."

You should have seen the look on her face. "Curt, you're are not in the desert anymore and you don't have to dig a hole and use the back yard. There's a nice clean toilet in the house."

I put the shovel down. "Just joking!" I said, and we started laughing.

Sadly, once I got back to Fort Sill, I started drinking heavily every chance I got to cover up my mental pain from the war and from missing my best buddy Tommy. Wolf and I became closer friends. I spent a lot of time shooting pool at his house and drinking. I was increasingly going out to the clubs and sleeping with more and more women, trying to cover my pain and satisfy my addictions. I'd be a wealthy man if I had all of the money I spent at strip joints and on alcohol and cigarettes.

CHAPTER 18

# TRAIN-ING WRECK

In August 1991 I had just gotten back to base after healing from my second left knee surgery. I went through the war with my cartilage torn pretty bad, but I survived. At the base, I was informed that we were going to NTC, the National Training Center, in the Mojave Desert. I thought, "Why in the world do we need more desert training when we just got back from a desert war three months ago?" But I couldn't do anything about it except go and make the best of training in the hot desert. At least I was on American soil this time. At NTC I was driving an M578 VTR, a track recovery vehicle, and Wolf was my assistant. He rode up in the turret to help watch where we were going and man the 50-caliber machine gun. The VTR weighs 53,000 pounds and we were pulling an M109 howitzer weighing 55,000 pounds.

At three o'clock in the morning we were driving through a small mountain range to work on a broken down howitzer. A mountain hid the moonlight and the tank trail had about a forty-degree downhill grade. Nobody is crazy enough to stop in the middle of a tank trail, especially in the dark. Or so I thought. I was wrong. The moonlight cracked through the mountains and Wolf yelled "HMVV!" at the same time I saw it. The HMVV wasn't clearing off the trail and there were only two options: veer to the side and hope for the best or try to stop. But we were too close to the HMVV. Its driver was asleep and he didn't realize he had parked on a tank trail. If we hit it, it could kill everyone in and around the HMVV (five men, it turned out). I yelled, "God, help us!"

I slammed on the brakes and pulled down on the gear shift as hard as I could. I knew it wouldn't work. You can't stop 100,000 pounds of vehicle in 20 or 30 yards. But all of a sudden, "Wham!" We stopped. We went flying inside the vehicle. My neck and back were instantly hurting me, but I didn't have time to worry about them because I was worried about Wolf. I couldn't afford to lose another close buddy. He had bruises on his head from being thrown around the 50-calibre mount, but he looked like he would be OK. I helped him out of the vehicle and saw that we were within three feet of the HMVV. Wolf and I limped the vehicle back to the motor pool to work on the damage from the howitzer rear-ending the VTR when we had stopped. We were both hurting pretty bad, but because we were young and invincible we thought we were OK.

After time passed we found out differently. Several years later, after I got out of the army, I was having trouble walking and using my left arm and hand. I had severe pain going through my gut, arm and left leg. I kept going back to the VA and they said that it was just muscle spasms due to degenerative disc disease. They said my walking problems were due to my bad knee. In reality, during the accident I fractured the T11 and the T12 in my spine and my L5 S1 disc was herniated, eventually ending up bone to bone. The same thing happened to my neck at C4 and C5. But I didn't know all of that for several more

93

years. The VA just kept telling me that I had fibromyalgia and muscle spasms.

After NTC I went back to Fort Sill. My life didn't change a bit. I went to church and church events, but mostly just to meet some good girls. I kept asking God to give me a good woman. However, I didn't want to change my lifestyle. I kept partying and doing what I had always done. I started living in a rental room in a woman's huge home, along with several other soldiers and strippers. I met a girl I really liked who worked at the strip joint that I frequented. She moved into the house with me. I thought I had fallen in love with her and asked her to marry me. But it wasn't love, it was just lust. We were engaged on Valentine's Day of 1992, the same day I got out of the army.

Once I got out, I tried find a job in Lawton, Oklahoma so we could keep our rental room, but I kept getting turned down. My mom kept saying to me, "Curtis, you need to re-think this relationship and this marriage." She didn't even know she was a stripper. I fell deeper in lust with her and I was sexually and emotionally attached in a bad way.

I finally got a job offer. TWA's main airplane maintenance facility in Kansas City offered to pay my way through their maintenance school and employ me immediately afterward. I was so excited and I kept trying to call my fiancée. But I couldn't locate her. Nobody knew where she was. My heart was in my stomach because I couldn't get in touch with her. TWA suggested that I stay in Kansas City a few days to get all the paperwork done and find a place to live. They were even going to give me work while I was going to their school.

But I walked away from the whole thing. I was distraught because I couldn't get in touch with my fiancée. I ended up flying back home and, boy, was I broken during that flight. I just knew something was wrong.

I got back to Lawton, to the house where I rented a room. She wasn't there and was nowhere to be found. I was so broken that I couldn't think straight at all. I had turned down the opportunity of a lifetime and now I couldn't even find my fiancée. A couple of days later she showed up, wanting to have sex with me. I was so glad to see her and we went to bed. Afterward, she told me that she found someone else and that she aborted my baby in order to be with him. I should have known this would happen. She had done the exact same thing to her boyfriend prior to me. But I had overlooked it because I was too sexually and emotionally involved. Addictions can not only ruin your life; they can even cost you someone you would have raised and loved life with also.

I felt horribly lonely and broken. My heart was getting as hard as a rock and my life was falling apart. Sadly, I still didn't surrender to God, even though deep down I knew that He was the only way. I was so mad and angry that I kept blaming God for everything that was happening. Most of my circumstances, though, were due to the bad choices that I kept making. I kept blaming God for Tommy's death and the death of my child. I was also angry at Him because I had to watch my mom die a slow and painful death.

My body reacted to all I was going through. I kept coughing up blood and losing weight and I felt drained all of the time. I went from my normal weight of 195 pounds to 150 pounds. My sister-in-law Becky even asked me if I had AIDS. Thank God I didn't, although not because I had been sexually safe.

One night I was staying at my parents' house when I overheard my mom talking to my dad. "My son didn't come back from the war," she said. "This is not the son I knew. And I know he is really sick."

I finally got a good job working as an operations manager at

LTL Trucking Company in OKC. I was so excited about the job and the good pay. I worked a lot of hours, and the more I worked the better that I felt mentally. Being at work helped me block out things that I didn't want to deal with.

In addition to working many hours, I played many hours. I was still going to the bars and strip joints, and it just got worse and worse. Somehow I thought that partying and women, as well as working, would enable me to forget all I had gone through. And all I was going through with my health and my mother's health.

Late one night I was supposed to meet a stripper at a restaurant. As I sat waiting, something in my head said, "This is enough. You have to make some changes."

She didn't show at the restaurant. So I went to another one to eat and I met this really nice waitress. We talked and decided to go out on a date. I was so proud of myself for finally meeting a woman somewhere other than a bar or a strip joint.

The evening we went out, we both drank a lot and I handled the relationship just like I did every other one. We immediately slept together. I quickly became both sexually and emotionally dependent on her. I wanted a real relationship so badly.

Then she told me she was married and had children. I knew in my heart that I needed to run, but instead I justified everything that she and I were doing. I just knew it could work. She left her husband and we got engaged.

It seemed like I'd never learn.

CHAPTER 19

# MOM

By this time my mom had been in the hospital in ICU for over a month and was on a breathing tube. Things happened in the hospital that show me that God was still working on my heart. On the day they put the breathing tube in my mom, she said to me without any struggle: "Son, don't worry. I know that I will see my children in heaven one day and it will be forever."

My mom was a nurse. She knew everything that was happening with her and it made me so sick to watch her slowly die. Yet her faith didn't waiver at all. The doctors were amazed at how clearly she was able to tell me what she told me.

Another time I was walking down to Mom's room in ICU and I heard some singing. I knew that it had to be my sister, Carla, singing to Mom. I got down there and Mom had plugged her trachea off and was singing Christian songs with my sister with every breath that she could grasp.

One of the most heartbreaking moments of my mom being in the hospital came when Mom couldn't talk with the breathing tube. She was still able to write down what she wanted to say. But eventually she couldn't even write. She would look up at me and want me to read her lips and tell people what she was saying. I was so brokenhearted because I was not able to read lips anymore. I told her that and she looked at me and smiled and I was able to understand it when she lipped, "It is OK, Son. I love you." She never stopped telling us that she loved us.

My fiancée and I had lived together about nine months in OKC when one night I felt like I was asleep, but I knew that God was speaking to me. I was arguing with God and I kept telling Him to heal my mom. He told me she was coming home to be in heaven that day. I said, "Why God? Why don't you heal my mother? My mom has always loved you and she is a wonderful person." God told me that it was time for her to come home now and that one day I would understand.

I came to my senses and I looked over to my fiancée and said, "I was just now dreaming that I was arguing with God about my mom."

She said, "You weren't dreaming. You were sitting up straight in bed with your eyes wide open and talking with Him."

My fiancée's parents were great people and strong Christ followers. So was her husband. The next day I kept going over what God had told me. I wondered why He bothered telling me this when I kept living a very sinful life and I refused to turn to Him.

My mom kept telling us to make things right with God and we would never go wrong. I felt in my mind that the only way to do this was to get married, but I learned much later that it was right before me the whole time.

Mom's best friend from childhood, Quetta, didn't leave her side. She was there when Mom went to be with the Lord. I was spending the evening with my fiancée, but I never quit thinking about what God had spoken to me. I knew deep down that

Mom was going to be with Him that day.

I got a phone call from Quetta telling me to get up to the hospital. We rushed there and I got by my mom's side and held her hand while they were working on her. Then they said that she was gone. I was all cried out. I had just had an encounter with the living God and He told me that this was going to happen, and it happened the very day He told me it would.

I spent some time with my mom's body and told her goodbye and I looked up to heaven as Quetta, my fiancée and I walked to the parking lot.

Quetta and I drove back to Hinton, to Mom and Dad's home. We talked about good memories the whole way. I started having thoughts that the reason God would not heal my mom was because I was living in an adulterous affair. I really didn't want to go to her funeral. It felt like I was back in a war zone again and the battle was right in front of me. But I pulled through. I went.

*CHAPTER 20*

# DOWNHILL

My fiancée and I were very convicted about our sin and we genuinely wanted to get things right with God. I really thought that would change everything. Her first husband had remarried. So, after living together almost two years, we got married also. But we were experiencing a lot of pressure in life. We both worked very long hours and when we weren't working, we were caring for her kids. Oh, yeah, I didn't mention that, did I? We had the children.

Under these circumstances, I could see more and more of my dad coming out in me. I was a horrible person to be around. I tried to be fun to be with, but things were going on with my mind and health that I didn't have any idea how to fix. And despite having wanted to get right with God, my spiritual condition wasn't particularly good, either. My back got worse and I had to have another surgery on my knee. The only emotional outlet I seemed to have was working long hours and being away from my new family. Eventually my health got bad enough that I wasn't able to work. I was granted funds by the VA to go back to college. We fixed up a house with the intention of buying it, but then the owner died and our finances crashed. We packed up and moved to Belton, Texas to live by my brother Dewayne and his wife Becky. We all became very close and had a lot of fun together.

But then everything fell apart. I had gone to the Temple, Texas VA for severe stomach pain, but they said they couldn't find anything wrong with me. A few days later, I woke up and couldn't stand up straight. I could hardly walk. I went to the bathroom and passed a lot of blood and then I went to the sink and I started vomiting acid and blood. My wife rushed me to the hospital. I almost bled out, but the doctors couldn't figure out where it was coming from.

I was in the hospital for many days having tests and blood transfusions. I felt like my heart was going to explode when it was fighting to find blood to pump through my veins. I was weak and sick to my stomach and my head was pounding, but it was my brother Dewayne who suddenly concerned me. I looked over at him late one night and I saw tears rolling down his cheeks as he tried to work a crossword puzzle. I mustered up the strength to ask him if he was OK. He said, "Little brother, I thought I was going to lose you at war and we just lost our mom and I can't lose you now."

I told him about a little man in a cartoon who said, "I can't die because I have too much to do and I'm way too far behind." I said, "Brother, I love you and I'm not going to die. It's going to be OK."

I never realized how near death I really was at the time and as I look back it really reminds me that God was with me. When they admitted me into the hospital I had less than a quarter of my blood left in my body.

My life took a drastic turn at this point. I was always in and out of the hospital due to bleeding and constant nausea with severe nerve pain and abdominal pain that was out of this world.

The sickness and weakness would not go away. They ran test after test after test. They also did exploratory surgeries to see if they could find out what was going on. Finally, they realized that it was the chemicals that I had been exposed to in the Middle East that were causing my problems.

On top of all of this, my dad's health had drastically turned for the worse. Dad was on his death bed several times. I was so fearful of losing my dad because we had just gotten really close not long before this.

The illness caused me to hurt even more and kept my nerves fired all the time. Then we learned that I had Post Traumatic Stress Disorder (PTSD) along with the illness and the spine issues. I had already had five left knee surgeries. I didn't know how severe my spine and neck injuries were for quite some time.

I went through severe nausea for several years along with severe abdominal pain. Finally, they did an ultrasound from inside my stomach to see if my gallbladder was functioning and they found it was enlarged. When they removed it, they asked for my permission to run tests on it because it was almost all mush and they hadn't seen anything like it before. They attributed the condition of my gallbladder to the chemicals that I had been exposed to in the Gulf War.

I truly felt that God was punishing me for the things that I had done. I could never forgive myself for what I had done to my wife, her first husband, and her children.

The doctors had me on Fentanyl, Vicodin, Soma, promethazine, Ativan, Prozac, phenobarbital, and Oxycontin to control the pain and constant nausea. I became extremely addicted to them and I would use them to try and cover the emotional, physical and spiritual pain that I was dealing with.

I eventually tried to take my life, but my wife got me to the hospital and they sent me to the VA suicide unit in Waco for several days. I was an emotional basket case, not a person that you wanted to be around.

My wife and I eventually divorced because of my addictions and the PTSD. I was trying to cover the pains of war and my mom and my illness by taking more and more medications and it nearly destroyed me. It did destroy our marriage.

Some things from that period have always stuck in my mind. One was my wife telling me she could not and would not be married to somebody that was disabled for life.

That stung badly. I was always thinking that the misery from the adultery, bad marriage and illness was God's revenge because of the things I had done and who I had become.

As I look back, I see God working in all of this, even when it looked like there was no hope for me at all. I felt like it was all my fault and that I had ruined a family and married the woman that I had an adulterous affair with, and that God did not and would not have anything to do with me. So now I tried to cover everything up with meds even more because now I was having to face the divorce and rejection.

The divorce was finalized in April of 2004. I told myself that I was finally free, but, boy, was I wrong. Eventually I started to go to church on my own and I started feeling bad about the divorce. I even started trying to take less medication. I was beginning to seek God in a serious way for the first time in my life, and what a journey it became.

I truly felt that God wanted me to reconcile with her. I started contacting her again and we even got together a few times. I later learned that God just wanted me to sincerely humble myself and ask for forgiveness from her and the children. God kept speaking to my heart, telling me that it was not about what she had done to me, but learning to forgive instead. I started realizing that I had been a horrible person and that illness and pain and medication abuse were not an excuse. I had become the dad I knew as a child and probably worse. I looked back at the nine years we had been married and I started thinking about when my dad literally got down on his knees and asked me for forgiveness for the dad or lack of thereof that he was when I was growing up. God built an awesome bond between my dad and me and I am so blessed that it happened.

I got a call from my ex-wife and she was broken. I tried to comfort her and she asked if we could just go out for dinner. I said yes. We met at a restaurant in OKC and had a nice dinner and she started telling me about this man that she was dating that was married. She told me that she didn't love me anymore and though the sex had been good, the marriage had not been.

It made me feel like dirt.

God was showing me once again my relationship was built on sexual pleasure and not on Him. Yes, we went to church all of the time and I was seeking God, but deep down I felt inadequate for God and I later realized that I was. I felt like her seeing this married man was my fault and that our marriage had meant nothing to her. The rejection I felt that night was more overwhelming than anything that I had felt before. I also thought about how I had hurt her children and first husband by having an adulterous affair with her and how I could never do anything to change it.

I was one broken dude. I knew I needed a Savior, and needed one right then. I had tried to make things right with God for many years. I couldn't seem to figure out the truth that was right before me, that I simply needed Jesus as my Savior. Instead, I kept trying to make myself feel better with the medications that the doctors gave me. I even shopped around to multiple doctors to get more. After I left the restaurant that night, I became so nauseated. For weeks I felt suicidal. Finally, I was ready to surrender. I was tired of holding onto the sin that had been destroying me up to this point in my life.

I had a close friend, Larry, a Vietnam vet. God had used him and his wife, Paula, to help keep me from taking my life. The pain of rejection, along with detoxing off of the medications the VA had me on, and losing everything I had that I thought was important to me, was destroying me inside. Larry and I were able to take a trip to California and I will never forget that time together. Larry helped me by talking to me about Jesus and how Jesus had helped him deal with the damage he had from war, both mentally and physically. He talked to me about forgiveness and God's love for us and how Jesus died for everything we did and not just some of it.

I loved this man like I had come to love my father and my buddy, Tommy. Larry was a soldier like me and he understood the pain I was dealing with. And he knew the answer to my problems. He said to me, "Bro, you need a Savior that you trust and Jesus is that Savior." We prayed and talked. This was the beginning of my walk with Jesus.

I was alone and having to live with my dad again. I felt like such a failure because I had to sell my house. I lost almost everything I owned. I was a broken and rejected man and I knew deep down that I needed a Savior. On Valentine's Day, I had another conversation with God. God spoke to my heart so strongly that it felt like He was verbally speaking to me. He said to me that I brought you out of Egypt and now you're heading for Gomorrah and if you don't turn back now you will be a pillar of salt. I knew enough Bible stories to know exactly what God was saying to me. I surrendered my life to Him that morning in the back bedroom of my dad's house.

I started going to church regularly and God's Word came alive to me. It was changing my life more and more every day and continues to do so today. I ended up getting the chance to ask my old family for forgiveness, but it wasn't in the way that I thought it would be. My ex-wife filed for a restraining order and I had a choice to go to court or not. I felt that God wanted me to. I prayed to God that He would speak in my place and that they would see Him and not me. The first words out of their mouths when they saw me at the courthouse were, "It doesn't even look like him." I knew I was supposed to be there and I knew that God was there with me.

When we went into the courtroom she started speaking. I knew that she was very angry at me for the person I had been and the things that I had done. I myself was very hurt inside for who I had been. It didn't matter to me what she had done to me anymore because God had changed my heart to focus on my relationship with Him, let go of the past, and unconditionally forgive. I knew deep down that God had forgiven me when I asked His Son Jesus into my heart and asked for forgiveness of all of my sins.

My ex-wife said many things about me. Many were not true, but it didn't make me angry with her. I was sorry that it was my sin that brought us to this place. When the judge asked if I had anything to say I humbly let God lead and control my tongue. All I could say, while tears were streaming down my face, was please forgive me and that I am very sorry for who I was and for what I had done.

The judge looked at me and said he found no fault in me and that I was a man of integrity. I knew that this was God, because I had not heard anything like that said about me in several years. I still remember talking to my ex-wife's mom about what had happened and she said to me, "Curtis, the most important marriage in your life is your marriage with Jesus Christ." Forgiveness is not a natural thing, it is a supernatural thing, and it can only be accomplished by recognizing what Jesus did on the cross.

While I was living with my dad, God set me free from my addiction to the medications, even though my dad took the same medications that I took. God's power trumped the power of addiction.

After I went to court, I went with several men from my church to Glorieta, New Mexico for a Men of Iron conference. I will never forget this young man singing a song called *Drugs or Jesus* at the conference. It opened my eyes even more and gave me a stronger will to stay away from the medications and to start trusting God with my mind, heart and soul.

CHAPTER 21

# NO CONDEMNATION

I went to work for an oil and gas company and traveled all over eastern Oklahoma. I was in church every time the doors were open and I faithfully read God's Word daily. In the town of Broken Arrow, an axle broke on my trailer and I had to drive the backhoe from Broken Arrow to Eufaula—a hundred miles! I sang praise songs and talked to God the whole hundred miles as that backhoe bounced alongside the highway. I got to the motel and sat at a picnic table and read God's Word. Afterward I took a shower, and in the shower God clearly spoke to my heart again. He told me that my son's name would be Micah and that he would be free of generational curses. God also spoke to my heart, saying that Micah's generation would be the generation that ushers in the King (Jesus). He didn't give me a date or time because that would be totally against God's Word.

I said to God, "I don't even have a girlfriend." I thought I was crazy!

I didn't even realize that Micah was a book in the Bible until I got out of the shower and looked. I started reading the book of Micah and God clearly showed me my life in it, how I had run from him and brought destruction into my life and how He redeemed me. Wow! I had been forgiven for *everything* that I had done.

There is nothing like God giving you revelation and knowing that the God of the universe is speaking directly to you through His Holy Word and that He wants a personal relationship with you. I went home to my dad's that weekend and told my sister, Carla, that God told me I was going to have a son. I figured she'd think that I was crazy.

But she just said, "What did God tell you to name him?"

"Micah."

I was so excited. I had been told for years that I couldn't have a child and that, if I did, the chemicals that I was exposed to in Iraq would cause birth defects. But I didn't fear this anymore. The only question was who was going to be the mother?

At my dad's house I decided to cancel an account I had with BigChurch.com, a Christian dating site. I was never home and most of the women on there were not godly women, anyway. The site even had my ex-wife as a 100 percent match for me. I got a good laugh from that one!

But I checked my email and I had one last message from a woman on BigChurch. Curiosity got the best of me and I opened it. The woman's name was Heather, she lived near Houston, and her email said, "Guard your heart with all diligence."

Boy, was my curiosity high now! Heather and I started trading emails. A week later we started texting each other and then we started talking on the phone every night. I was trying to be this super Christian because I knew that she was a godly woman and really loved Jesus like I did. My oldest brother Jerry said to me, "She knows where you stand spiritually, so now be yourself, dummy, before you blow it." So I started just being myself.

Heather told me that the Christian band Third Day was having a concert in Houston at Astroworld. "Would you like to go with me?" she asked. That was a no-brainer. I flew down to Houston on August 6, 2005. On the flight I saw the most incredible thing I'd ever seen: a huge rainbow in the shape of a full circle.

Heather picked me up at the airport and I immediately told her about the rainbow. We went to the concert and afterward just walked around the amusement park. I didn't even hold her hand; we just side-hugged. It was cool because we were building a godly relationship that honored Him. God had changed my heart and my desire was to fully please Him in my earthly relationships now.

I was so smitten with Heather that I even rode the parachute drop with her—without drugs! I had been off of medications for four months at this point. Heather and I went to church together and I told God I wanted a wife who was not afraid to worship Him. I could see my prayer being answered right before my eyes.

At the time I didn't have a job. I had been working for Arkla, a regional gas company, driving heavy equipment and cleaning out overgrown brush around high pressure gas lines. Unfortunately, I got poison ivy really bad and had a severely allergic reaction to it. That was the end of that job. I told Heather that I was willing to take a huge pay cut and substitute teach.

Within a week of our first date, however, Heather and I were both questioning this long-distance relationship. How could we actually make it work?

The next Friday, Heather was heading to Jacksonville, Texas to buy her grandma a new front door.

"The hard part," she told me, "is going to be finding someone trustworthy to install it."

I replied completely off the cuff. "All you have to do is ask."

"What did you say?" she asked. "You would drive 300 miles down here and do that?"

"Of course."

We agreed to meet at her grandma's house the next day. I only had one problem. I hadn't worked in a few weeks. As a result, I was dead broke.

I started praying immediately. "God, provide me the funds to go down there." It wasn't ten minutes later when I got a call from my nephew, Jason, whom I hadn't heard from in months. He wanted me to mow some oil well sites for him. He filled up my truck with gas and gave me enough money to get to Jacksonville and back, with enough left over to go out to eat a few times.

The next day we got the door installed, put up some safety rails around the front steps, sweated profusely in the humid heat, and had a lot of laughs. I never felt as welcome as I did being around Heather, her Grandma Violet, and her Aunt June. And Violet was thrilled with the door. It was such a blessing to be a part of that.

Heather and I went roller skating that night. It was a blast, but the nerve pain in my back and neck really got triggered. I didn't stop skating, though.

After we were done skating we went out on the big pier on Lake Jacksonville and looked up at the stars together and talked about God and our dreams. We kissed for the very first time on that pier. I just knew we had God's full approval. The next day we went to church and lunch, and then we both had to return to our homes.

When we were leaving we gave each other a small kiss and said goodbye. I remember her telling me that to love someone is a choice just like it is with choosing to love God. She started to drive off and I stopped her. I knew that God was telling me to tell her how I felt. I went up to her car and looked her in the eye and sincerely told her that I loved her.

When I returned to my dad's, God provided me an awesome job running an oilfield maintenance shop at nights. This job gave me the ability to fly to Houston and see Heather every weekend if I wanted. Heather and I traded off traveling between Houston and Oklahoma. One weekend when she came to Oklahoma, I had bought her a promise ring. We went to church and the message was on marriage. She told Aunt June that I gave her a promise ring. Aunt June asked, "What in the world is a promise ring?"

I wanted to ask Heather to marry me, especially after my dad said, "If you don't know if you want to marry each other in a month you will never really know." Heather and I both agreed with that statement.

Early one morning the next week, after I got off of work I went to the store and bought an engagement ring. I was just waiting for the right time and hoping that she would accept my proposal. I knew that I had made a lot of mistakes in life and that I was still walking through serious financial consequences because of my poor choices and my prior marriage, but I loved her.

God kept reminding me about what He says in Romans 8:1: "Therefore, there is now no condemnation for those who are in Christ Jesus." I knew that I was truly His child now.

CHAPTER 22

# HEATHER, AND THEN MICAH!

The next time Heather came to visit me in Oklahoma, we went to Fort Sill, Mount Scott, and The Holy City that afternoon after church. The Holy City was built by materials from Israel and it looks just like biblical days. It even has a makeshift Calvary Hill with three crosses on it. I had contemplated suicide after the war and a lady came up and talked to me and prayed with me at the bottom of the center cross. She talked me out of suicide.

Now I was sitting at the foot of this cross again as a true believer and Christ follower and I was there with my future wife. As we talked, I spilled out everything about myself. Heather just looked at me and said that she loved me no matter what. God knew that I needed to hear those words. I was so scared to share the mistakes that I had made in life and I just knew that she was going to walk away when I told her, but God had different plans. My sins were forgiven and this was a new life and a new walk for me. I started to catch on to forgiveness and what it really means.

Heather and I went to Medicine Park. We were near the dam

and started walking over a bridge. A man stopped and talked to us on the bridge. He told us how he and his wife had walked across the bridge sixty years ago and they married and lived a wonderful life together. We finished talking with him and then we walked just a few feet to the end of the bridge and turned around to see the old man. But he was nowhere to be found. We think that he was an angel, but only God knows. Heather didn't know that I was planning to ask her to marry me and God was lining up everything perfectly.

The next day we went to the OKC Bricktown Riverwalk to eat and I told Heather to close her eyes and when she opened them I was on my knees with an engagement ring asking her to marry me. And she said yes.

We got on the phone and told all our family members. Heather called Aunt June and told her that the difference between a promise ring and an engagement ring is about one week. So the wedding was on, and so was the planning. We considered going to Honduras, Fiji, Hawaii and many more places to get married and to spend our honeymoon. But the more we talked about it, the more deeply I felt that we should just keep our wedding and honeymoon close by. Then I got a phone call from my heartbroken bride-to-be. "I've been laid off work," she said, crying. Now I knew why God had given me that feeling. Soon thereafter, while visiting Grandma Violet together, Heather said, "Why don't we get married right here on the lake?" It was a great idea. Heather had grown up most of her life in Jacksonville and she has always loved Lake Jacksonville.

I called my nephew Mike, a pastor whom I hadn't seen in twenty years, and he agreed to do the ceremony. I found out that he lived just under an hour away from Jacksonville. God was in the middle of everything and it was so evident. Mike was so grateful to be asked to do our wedding ceremony and I was so grateful to have him do it.

The date was set for October 17, 2005. God provided everything we needed for the wedding and then some. Heather planned everything so perfectly. I could see that God had blessed me with a talented and beautiful woman who loved Him with all her heart.

When the ceremony started, Mike started talking about the rainbow and how God sent it as a reminder that He would never destroy the earth again with water. Then he spoke about the ring and how it is an endless circle and it cannot be broken without outside force. Mike didn't know about the circle rainbow I had seen the first time I went to see Heather, but Heather and I shared it with him during the wedding reception.

Can you say *only* God?

Heather then said a few things that really cracked us all up. She said that when I told her about the rainbow that she thought that I was going to say it was God telling us to get married. The funny thing is that I never even thought of that at all. I was just totally amazed at the rainbow I had seen. When Mike said what he said during our ceremony, God revealed to me what He was telling me from the beginning and it all made sense now.

I remember a verse that God showed Heather when I proposed. Isaiah 60:18 says: "No longer will violence be heard in your land, no ruin or destruction within your borders, but you will call your walls Salvation and your gates Praise."

We honored God during our courtship and with our marriage, but let me tell you something. You must hold on to what God speaks to your heart, because even when things look so dim and dark He still keeps His promise. But we must be committed to Him. Marriage is not an easy task, but it is worthwhile one and, most importantly, we must honor God in our journey.

Heather and I were deeply in love and intimacy which created this almost euphoric atmosphere all around. This euphoria was better than any medication that I had ever taken. We had been married right at one month when we found out that Micah was on his way. We had only dated two and a half months before we got married and now we had been married one month and our lives were about to change drastically. I was seeing God's Word that He had spoken to my heart play out right before my eyes. I didn't think that it would happen this quickly, but God knew what He was doing.

I look back and laugh at Grandma Brown when she thought that we had been doing hanky-panky before marriage. But I knew that for the first time in a relationship I had truly done things the way God wanted me to do them. It concerned me at first when some people thought that we had done things before our marriage, but if they would just do the math they would see that we were truly obedient during our courtship.

I had moved to Houston when we got married and did some side jobs for a while, but due to the consequences of our prior divorces we were having difficulty financing a home. We got a little impatient, or should I say a lot impatient. Heather was dealing with hormonal changes and the challenges that come with being pregnant and I was learning to deal with her changes too.

We were so excited knowing that we were going to be parents. But I was anxious as well, wondering what kind of father I would be. My dad called us daily and asked Heather to put the phone to her belly so that he could tell Micah that Papa loved him. I could never express the pride I had knowing that I was going to be a father, but also seeing my father be a father to me and encourage me and showing the love for a grandson that he had not yet seen was amazing.

We have such a love for our children and an excitement along with anticipation of their arrival even before we ever see their faces. They are nourished and taken care of from the start. That reminds me of our relationship with God. It reminds me how as Christ followers we have an excitement and anticipation of seeing Him and a love for Him without ever seeing His face.

I thought of Micah being in Heather's belly and I knew that one day I would hold him and nurture him and teach him and, most importantly, love him. Everything around me pointed to that little baby that God blessed my wonderful wife Heather and me with.

I can still hear my friend Larry saying to me, "Heather, Heather, Heather! All I hear is Heather, Heather, Heather!" We would crack up laughing when he did that.

One night Larry called me as I was driving across Houston. He said he had been having chest pains and that he was really tired. I prayed with him. He said he was ready to check out of this motel, but he had to wait until God let him turn in his keys. I tried to encourage him, but I could tell that he was really tired from the liver damage he had sustained from Agent Orange and the broken-up body that he had.

Heather and I had laid down to go to sleep that night when we got a call from Paula. She said, "Curtis, I am calling you first because I know Larry would want me to. Larry has gone to be with Jesus." I was brokenhearted, but at the same time I had peace because I knew that my wonderful friend was at the feet of Jesus and he was not hurting anymore.

We drove to Larry's funeral and I had the honor of being a pall bearer. I did OK until Taps was played. Then his sister introduced herself to me and said, "My brother loved you more than you will ever know." I leaned on Heather and broke down crying at that point.

Heather's pregnancy was going well. While we were at Heather's OB/GYN, even before the doctor told us it was a boy we had told her that his name was Micah David. She asked, "How in the world did you know it was a boy? You were so sure you had already picked out a boy's name." We shared with her that we felt that God had spoken to our hearts and told us that we would have a boy and to name him Micah, and that we added the David.

We later learned that in Hebrew Micah means *who is like our God* and David means *beloved friend*. What a challenge we would have raising this little guy and what a responsibility to raise him in a way that honored God. I realized more than ever that we are at war and it's not for the faint of heart. Although we know who wins the battle, we still must faithfully walk across the battlefield in obedience.

At this point, Heather and I were looking for a home in the Houston area, either to buy or a lease purchase. But we hadn't found anything yet that was right. We went to Jacksonville, Texas to visit Grandma Violet. My cousin Mike introduced me to a man who mentioned an A&P mechanic course at Letourneau University in Longview, Texas. I had been working on getting the funding to go back to school and work on airplanes while living in Houston, but I had not heard anything yet. Heather and I checked out Letourneau and I decided I wanted to pursue aeronautics engineering there. I just had to convince the VA to fund it.

We decided to move to northeast Texas, halfway between LeTourneau in Longview and Grandma Violet in Jacksonville. That placed us in Henderson, half an hour from both. We found a huge home in Henderson and the owner was willing to owner finance. It was a 3450 square-foot prairie style home. (You can get an amazing amount of house for the money in East Texas!) We had a vision and we just knew that God was directing us to Letourneau and to this home. I had remodeled a few homes in my past, but nothing as big as this home. Even though it was so big, we had limited places to put our stuff because of the work that the house needed.

We were excited about everything that was happening. Heather was due to have Micah in less than three months. My mother-in-law, Donna, had started introducing us to natural medicine. This meant natural child birth as well.

We wanted the very best for Micah as he came into this world and after he arrived. My cousin Sue, who is a mid-wife, was a huge blessing and she was able to answer questions. It was Sunday morning, July 30, 2006 and we were getting ready for church. We attended church at Westminster Bible Church in Henderson, Texas. We were so blessed to be there at this time in our lives. Heather told me that she felt a little under the weather when we were getting ready for church and so I called Papa Wess (Weslie Verden) and told him that we would probably be a little late. Papa Wess said that he would be praying for us and that he would see us next week. I thought we would still go to church, but he was right. The day was bittersweet for me as we soon learned two things: Heather was in labor, and my dad was in the hospital from a stroke. I was very excited about Micah being on his way, but at the same time I was fearful that I was going to lose my dad. I badly wanted my dad to see his newest grandson and my heart was torn.

Heather was a trooper through the labor. Being at a birthing center was so much better than being in a hospital. We arrived at the birthing center at around ten in the morning and Heather gave birth to Micah that night around 8:30. I got to witness the whole thing. My heart was in my throat the whole time. When Heather was having trouble pushing the mid-wife had her squat like an Indian squaw and out Micah came. I got to cut the cord and hold him with my wife. Wow! We were parents and God had proven Himself to me. The promise that He gave me was in my arms and he was healthy as a horse. The midwife had Heather get in a warm bath with natural herbs and Micah was just floating in the bath as if he was at home. It was so cool watching my life change before my eyes. And I hadn't been the only one there for Micah's birth. So were Grandma Violet, Aunt June Rose, Grandma Miller, and my mother-in-law Donna.

I called to tell my stepmom, Ruby, that I was a daddy to a seven-pound, two-ounce baby boy. To my relief, she reported that my dad was doing much better.

We drove home that night and Micah slept on my chest. He actually slept on my chest for the first two weeks of his life while Heather was healing and getting stronger.

## CHAPTER 23

# DAD

The break from our trials was short-lived. I started having severe abdominal pains for the first time in several years. We went to the emergency room at the hospital in Henderson. They wanted to do surgery, but we hesitated and told them we would decide in the morning.

The next morning I was still hurting badly, so Papa Wess drove us to Good Shepherd Hospital in Longview. We were the youngest couple in our church and it was amazing to see these wonderful people that were so full of love and life step up and help us. I was admitted to the hospital and they removed my appendix, even though they said that it looked OK. But I continued to have the left arm pain and abdominal pain, and it continued to get worse. Micah was about a month old when, as I was sitting on the roof of our home nailing a board, I lost all continence. Heather immediately took me to the VA clinic in Longview. They sent me to the Shreveport VA by ambulance. They did X-rays and an MRI, but eventually said they couldn't find anything. This wasn't the first (or the last) time the VA said that there was nothing wrong.

In addition to the abdominal pain, I couldn't feel my fingers on my left hand and I was losing use of it. My left leg was giving me more and more trouble. I had had pain between my shoulder blades since the tank accident in the Mojave Desert. I had also had my leg pain since then.

Heather and I went to a routine doctor's appointment where we found out that T11 & T12 in my thoracic spine had been broken at one time. They couldn't answer the questions about my left arm and hand, shoulder blade pain, and left leg. The only answer we could get was degenerative joint disease of the lumbar spine. That had been diagnosed years before.

We ended up going to a spine surgeon. We paid out of our own pocket and found out that C4 & C5 were bone to bone and the disc was completely herniated. We took the results to the VA in Shreveport, but they simply repeated the response of the VA in Temple. They gave me pain medicine. We kept fighting with them to get them to pay for me to get my neck fixed, but they kept refusing to do so.

One positive development was that while all of this was happening, my dad and I spoke every day. He asked me to move back home to Hinton, but I told him that for the first time in my life I knew that I was where God wanted me to be. He said, "Son, never change that. Always be where God wants you to be."

When Micah was three months old, we drove to Oklahoma to see my dad. I had no idea 385 miles could take so long and be so draining. Having an infant changed travel. Actually, having an infant changed everything.

We got to my sister's at ten at night and drove to my dad's the next morning. My brother Jerry was there. So was an ambulance. They were loading Dad into it. My heart fell. This was the first time that he was going to see his new grandson and now I didn't even know if he was going to make it home.

By the grace of God, though, he got to come home the next day. We spent time with him and he played with Micah. It was a precious time that I will never forget. We continued to grow as parents and build relationships in the community. And though we could see my health going downhill, we continued to work on the old house we had bought. I talked to my dad daily and he would tell me what Dr. Charles Stanley had taught on his TV program that day. God is so amazing. I found almost every day that God had been speaking to my heart about the same thing that he was showing my dad through Dr. Stanley.

Dad called one day in January 2007. "Son, I need you guys to come up here ASAP." I knew it couldn't be good and I was really concerned. I remembered how skinny he was the last time I had been there and I could picture him having lost even more weight. Heather and loaded up everything to make the long trip in the freezing cold of winter while praying that the roads would be clear. After several hours of driving we arrived at my sister's house at 11:00 p.m. Dad called and I told him we'd be there first thing in the morning.

"I need you to come now, Son."

We left Micah with my sister and headed over. He was so excited to see us and then he sprang the news.

"They put me on hospice today."

"What?" I replied.

"They are going to keep me comfortable and pain free."

The first thing that came to my mind, and Heather's, was that they were going to drug him to death. And with him being so addicted to narcotics, he would ask for all he could get. Dad had been on narcotics as long as I could remember and they were finally causing his body to simply shut down. He was very coherent that night, though.

He wasn't the next day. When we took Micah over to see Papa, he was completely out of it. It broke my heart to see Dad this way. It reminded me of how I had seen him several times growing up. The difference this time was that he was near death. I knew that he was hurting and needed pain meds, but he didn't need someone to legally overdose him.

As if my constant physical pain was not enough, I could now see the end of my dad's life coming quickly. It started bringing back memories of war, knowing that's where my injuries had come from, and that I lost my best buddy during the war, and my mom right after the war. I felt truly broken, but Heather helped me keep things in perspective and continually prayed for me and encouraged me.

When we drove away from my dad's to return home, we had gone just one block when Heather asked, "Honey, is there anything that you need to say to your dad?"

"There are a lot of things I'd like to say, but only one crucial thing comes to mind."

She held my hand and said, "Then drive back to your dad's house right now and tell him what is on your heart, because we both know this is the last time that you are going to see him this side of heaven."

I turned around, drove back, and Heather, Micah and I went inside the house. I helped Dad hold Micah and though he was very medicated, he was smiling at him. And I got the chance to tell him something that I never in my life imagined I would ever be able to say. You see, I had forgiven my dad for everything through the love of Jesus and through Jesus changing my heart towards my dad. So I said to him, "Daddy, I want you to know that you have become more than just a father to me, you have become my very best friend."

Those words came from the bottom of my heart and I meant

them with all of my heart. Daddy smiled and whispered with what little strength he still had, "I love you dearly, Son."

Heather went over to him and held his hand and hugged him. "Dad," she said, "I will see you at the feet of Jesus." He smiled at her and nodded and said, "I love you, too." We finally started the drive home to Henderson and I felt like I was in a fog the whole trip. I knew it was the last time I would see my father alive. We had talked and talked, but I can't remember what we talked about. It wasn't a week later when we got a call from my sister and brother Dewayne. "You need to come up now if you want to see Dad alive again." I knew Dad wouldn't know me at that point, nor would he hear me if I was there. I also knew that my brother and sister needed to be there with him. So we just waited.

I got a call the next morning that Dad had gone to be with the Lord. I knew it before the phone ever rang, though. I had gotten up to spend time with God that morning and when I went to pray for Dad I knew that there was no need to pray because he was no longer with us. I talked to my Papa Brown and he had the exact same experience.

The funeral arrangements my brothers Jerry and Dewayne and my sister Carla agreed on didn't sit well with me. They planned to bury Dad beside Mom and have a hole deep enough for my step-mom to be buried on top of him when she passed. Not that I didn't love my stepmom, but I didn't think it was respectful to my mom and it didn't sound right to have him dug up later on. They didn't plan to have a service at the church. Dad had asked me to have his service at First Baptist Church, but they decided to have it at the funeral home because of the cost. I felt devastated and broken even more.

So Heather and I prayed. The next day we got a call and found out that the church was working with us on the cost and that a separate plot had been provided to bury my step-mom in when she passed. God worked everything out once again.

God provided beautiful weather on that late January day and we all had peace from Him. As we went with Dad's coffin to the gravesite, we all reminisced and laughed about things Dad said and did. We were all learning to forgive our dad for the things he had done as we grew up.

## CHAPTER 24

# IN A MEDICATED FOG

I heard someone says once: If you want to hear God laugh, tell Him your plans. I have found this to be so true!

Heather and I had planned to quickly restore our big home and then enjoy it and share it with others. This did happen to some extent, but for the most part our home became our own personal battle zone. It wasn't just a battle against the world; it was against each other. I had started taking pain medications once again because of the spinal injuries. What I didn't realize was that I had lost my ability to reason with God or my wife and son. My disobedience was getting back on the medications and not trusting God to see me through these injuries. This created a battle zone both within my own heart and within our home. I loved my wife and she loved me, but I didn't see what the medications were doing to me. I wasn't the person that my wife had married as long as I allowed these medications to rule my life. I thought that I was OK because the VA put me on Tramadol and told me it wasn't an addictive narcotic, yet my ability to reason and how I responded to every situation was changing without me even noticing it.

I was being programmed by the world and its ways once again. I was genuinely seeking God, but I was also listening to others who had had injuries and told me they were pain-free. Yet they were continuing to take narcotics.

Primarily, I was trusting the doctors, not God. Not that I am against doctors—not at all. However, for me and my family, at this time in our lives, God had a better way. There were ways to heal naturally which would have prevented addiction.

As men we are fallible and we make mistakes. Sadly, most of the time we look out for our own best interest. My father was addicted to porn, pain medications, alcohol and tobacco. God had called him to preach his Word when we moved to Oklahoma, yet he refused to do so and the effect on our family was devastating. Like King Saul in the Old Testament, Dad did not take out the enemy completely as God had called him to do. So the enemy grew and spread throughout our household. Just as King David lost his family to an enemy that should have been destroyed by the king before him, I was losing my family to the enemy because of disobedience on my part.

I was overwhelmed by all of the work that we were doing on our home, by the severe chronic pain that I was dealing with day and night, and by the stress of Heather and I battling with each other. I had lost vision of the rainbow that God showed in the sky the day I met Heather, and she had lost vision of the Scripture that God had given her about no more destruction.

We had become each other's enemies, yet in reality we were not enemies at all. We were both God's children. We both loved God and had Jesus in our hearts, but we started focusing on each other's faults rather than allowing God to heal us.

Heather was doing everything she knew to do to help me, but I was so distraught and angry that I was impossible to deal with. In addition to the chronic pain and my arm, hand, and leg issues, I could no longer stand very long. Heather looked high and low for doctors to help me as well as natural means to help.

The stronger the pain got the more medications I used, and the more disoriented I got without realizing it. I was unable to sleep at night because of the severe pain. During the day when I would try to sit and relax, the pain was still excruciating. The pain meds were not helping at all, yet they clouded my ability to reason and think straight. I didn't realize I was continuing to hurt myself more and more. The more I hurt myself the more pain medicine I took and the more I pain meds I took the more I hurt myself. It became a vicious cycle.

Heather became terribly frustrated and I became terribly frustrated because I thought she was continually against me and just didn't understand. We got to the point where we couldn't even talk normally with each other anymore. Everything seemed to turn into a fight. I couldn't communicate with her without throwing emotional punches and accusing her of yelling at me and arguing with me. I didn't understand the side effects of these medications, nor did I see the changes they were making in my actions and my reactions, along with my ability to communicate properly.

We went to the VA numerous times. The neurosurgeon there, Dr. S, told Heather and I that there was nothing wrong and that since I had been on pain meds for so long I would never get off of them. Heather and I showed him the reports of two other doctors and the MRI readings which showed damage in my neck. We also showed him reports of the two vertebrae in my thoracic spine that had been broken. The VA had hidden injuries from me for many years, but now it was starting to come to light. However, Dr. S told us there was nothing he could do. We had only come to him for an opinion, he said.

We had come to him because we had to have his opinion to be able to have any option of getting repaired.

They kept putting me on stronger pain meds as well as increasing the number that I was taking every day. I kept getting more and more addicted. We kept begging the VA for help, and searching elsewhere as well, so I could get repaired, heal, and get off of all the pain medications. Our marriage was in shambles and my ability to be a husband and a father was failing. Due to the pain and weakness I couldn't hold my son. Or even his bottle.

*CHAPTER 25*

# HOPE

Heather and I started working with Rosemary Mason, an awesome patient's advocate at the Shreveport VA. Rosemary stood up for us and helped us fight. She spoke with Dr. P, the acting chief of staff at the hospital. One night in December of 2007, Dr. P called and told us he had a surgeon that was very competent. He was even a surgeon of the year.

The surgeon would eventually perform two surgeries on my neck and one on my lumbar spine. Heather and I were relieved and excited that this was finally going to come to an end. We were finally going to get some relief for my pain and for our family.

My surgery date was set for the middle of January 2008. On January 4, Heather and I were standing in our kitchen and I was holding Micah's bottle. I turned my head to say something to her and excruciating pain shot through my body and I dropped the bottle. Heather called the doctor and asked if there was any way we could speed up the surgery. It was rescheduled for two days later.

My cousin Mike and his wife Melinda kept Micah while I

went in for surgery in Shreveport. Dr. P's physician assistant came to see me after the surgery. She told me that the disc in my neck was completely gone and it had been bone to bone. Sadly, this had been the case for years, but neither the VA in Temple nor Oklahoma City diagnosed it. Or had they simply not told me about it, as they had hidden the fact that my spine had been broken in two places?

I got out of the hospital the next day feeling much better. Finally, I thought, this was the end of all of the chronic pain. Heather and I were very optimistic and excited. A few weeks later, we went back to Dr. P for my checkup. He said everything looked fine and told me to detox off of my medications cold turkey.

I was petrified. I had gone off my medications cold turkey before and I knew how horrific that could be. Heather started researching ways to ease my detox pains and sickness. Heather bought me oat straw tea and many supplements to help me through the detox process. She was by my side the whole way, even when I couldn't sleep or eat and even when I made a mess of myself. She prayed for me day and night and pleaded with God to help me through this.

We later found out that I could have had a heart attack going through detox like the doctor advised. I already have a heart condition called mitro valve prolapse. I'm sure the detox stressed my heart further, but we serve a bigger God than my heart.

On the third day of detox I woke up soaking wet in sweat, but I felt much better. Heather said, "It's time to go outside. It's such a beautiful day. Let's take Micah to the park." I was ready to go. We went to the park and the sun was shining bright and Micah was so excited to have me go play with him. I was thanking God over and over even while I was learning to deal with the mind fog that existed for some time because of the medications. When Micah would sleep on my lap or when he was in my arms, I would try to remember if my dad ever held me like that as a child. Sometimes I would cry because I couldn't remember that.

During this time, while I was spending time with Him, God reminded me once again of what He had spoken to me when I worked for TIPCO in Freeport, Texas. He had told me then that I would preach His Word. I brought this up to Heather and we were in agreement that God wanted me to be ordained. I talked with pastors Scott Rambo and Kenny Dean at The Bridge Fellowship in Sugar Land, Texas, where Heather and I had attended church before we moved to Henderson. I was ordained in April 2008 by The Bridge Fellowship. Roger Dauzat did my testimonial at my ordination. I am honored to call Roger my brother, my friend and my mentor.

Finally, I was pain free in God and peace was restored within our home once again. It was a great and exciting time and we enjoyed each other every day. My mind continued to get clearer and clearer as days passed. Heather was excited to have her husband back and I was excited to be back as a father and a husband once again.

I drew closer and closer to God and He gave me opportunities to share His Word at small churches in Northeast Texas. I didn't know what my future held, but I was seeking God for his direction for me and my family. We were thriving and growing together and growing with God. We were optimistic about our future and we continued to work on what seemed like a lifelong project in our huge 3800 square foot home.

*CHAPTER 26*

# BACK TO EGYPT

Then one day, out of the blue, I sneezed and my neck popped and the excruciating pain started all over again. Only it was worse than before and I became very nauseated. I was so afraid to tell Heather. I didn't want to disappoint her and we were all having such a wonderful day. I made it through the day, but I couldn't sleep that night because of the excruciating pain. It was shooting through my shoulder blades, down my left arm and shoulder and into my hand. And I had lost the strength in my arm again.

All I could think of was *here we go again*. My mind was filled once more with crazy thoughts. I was begging God, "Please don't allow us to go through this again." But I know God has our best interest at heart, and I know God allows things to happen to draw us close to Him. I've also learned that God will never leave us nor forsake us. Even when it seems that I'm alone, He is all around me.

I told Heather. I could see the frustration in her eyes and I could hear the brokenness in her voice. Her first words were, "God, please don't let us go through this again." Just like me.

Our greatest fears were the effect of any medications and the wait, wondering when this could be taken care of or if the VA would really take care of me.

I went to the emergency room at Good Shepherd Hospital in Longview. They said that they could tell that something was going on; however, all they could do was give me something to control the pain. I tried to get into my primary care doctor at the VA hospital in Shreveport, but the wait was extremely long. Heather and I used my Medicare and went directly to Dr. P, the neurosurgeon that did the surgery on my neck. He sent me to Dr. W, who performed a discogram on my neck.

I was already fearful because of the severe pain and loss of use of my left arm and left hand. Now I was going in for a procedure that scared me to death. A discogram consists of inserting needles into the disc or discs that are damaged and injecting dye and filling them to see how much damage there is while re-creating the pain. Dr. W didn't medicate me at all and he inserted four needles through the front of my neck into four levels of discs in my cervical spine. He found that the one below my neck fusion was also herniated and was leaking. Heather and I had to pay out of our pocket to get this procedure done.

We pleaded with the VA to pay for these procedures to find out what was going on, but they refused. We were so distraught because of all of the damage once again and the uncertainty that accompanied it, especially uncertainty about the medications' effect on me. The doctors put me back on methocarbamol, Neurontin, promethazine, Norco and Effexor. If we had only known the true side effects of all of these medications and the dangers they create emotionally, physically and spiritually.

Dr. W gave the test results to Dr. P and Dr. P contacted the VA. Once again we had to wait to go through Dr. S, the head neurosurgeon of the VA. Dr. S once again gave us his full dose of arrogance: we came to him for an opinion, and in his opinion there was nothing wrong. Rosemary was once again a godsend for us. She fought diligently to help us and so did Congressman Louie Gohmert, a man of integrity and a true man of God. He continues to fight on my behalf against the VA system to this very day.

The pain got so excruciating in October 2008 that I was admitted into the VA hospital in Shreveport and administered IV pain medications to control the pain. Heather and I were both so stressed because she had to drive over 80 miles each way to the hospital to see me with our two-year-old son Micah. At the same time, she was still trying to restore this huge home in a community where we hardly knew anyone. As I look back now I see God teaching me to trust Him more.

After I had been in the hospital for seven days, I finally looked at the results that Dr. P and Dr. W came up with and presented them to Dr. S as well as the Chief of Staff. The decision was made to allow me to go through fee-basis surgery at another hospital once again and have Dr. P repair my neck.

Less than two weeks later, Dr. P operated on my neck. The operation did not go as he had planned. Dr. P told Heather and me that he would remove the old plate from the first fusion, insert one for the damage of the other disc, and fuse it. After the surgery I woke up in my room and I was in excruciating pain which would not let up. On top of that, my anxiety was through the roof. I simply hadn't experienced this before.

Heather held my hand and prayed for me. The pain would not let up. Finally, we told the nurse that my pain was not under control. The nurse said I must have hit my pain button too many times (the one that released the medication) and I would simply have to wait before it would dispense more through the IV. Heather then noticed that my IV tube was not even plugged in to the port. I hadn't been getting any medication!

They started to actually give me some, but it still didn't control the pain. Or the anxiety. We knew something was wrong, but it would take nearly two years to finally find out what it was. During that time, I learned more and more where my trust really needed to be.

I was released from the hospital and I went home after picking up Micah from our cousins' house in Kilgore. What a blessing it was to have Mike and Melinda, Justin, Alicia, Amanda and Tyler in our lives and praying for us. God is so faithful to always provide and He provided us with family not too far away. I got off the pain medications once again for about a month. My lumbar spine and left leg started giving me excruciating pain and I was losing the ability to hold my bowels and my bladder.

Heather and I and Heather's mom started looking into more natural means to control the pain. But I started returning to the pain and anxiety medications for relief. Sadly, I was turning to them instead of trusting God's way of healing. This created a lot of discontent between Heather and me and a wall of distrust for many years.

While on the medications I couldn't tell you what the truth was. I thought the medications were helping me, yet they were hindering and delaying my healing process and creating more damage between me and Heather, Micah, and the rest of my family. The VA once again gave me the runaround. I still trusted Dr. P and I went to him. He sent me back for a discogram with Dr. W on my lumbar spine. I watched them stick a needle through my side all the way into the middle of my body into my spine. We found out that my L5 S1 was bone to bone because the disc was badly herniated.

For once, the VA acted quickly. In January 2009, Dr. P did a T-lift on my lumbar spine at L5 S1. I was released and went home in excruciating pain, but that was to be expected because of the surgery that was performed. However, my left foot kept swelling and I was unable to move it. My left arm, left shoulder and left hand were continuing to hurt and so were my shoulder blades. And now the pain was starting on my right side. I was even starting to have issues with swallowing and talking. We didn't know if it was the medications, nerve damage, or both.

After my second neck surgery and my lumbar surgery I never was able to get off pain medications. Sadly, I was able to justify all of the med use because of the pain.

One day in March 2009 I was gently walking down our stairs when my left leg gave out and I tumbled to the bottom. Heather was there waiting for me and saw it happen. When I looked up, tears were rolling down her face. I could see the fear in her eyes.

We had to go to the emergency room at the VA hospital in Shreveport and they admitted me. They had me on IV medications to control the pain. One doctor I saw said my MRI showed something wrong in my lumbar spine, but he wasn't sure what. I didn't see him again. Every other doctor said nothing was wrong, that it was a pain management issue, and that they were keeping me on strong IV meds to control the pain.

The addiction was roaring and this monster was uncontrollable once again. They did injections in my neck over and over and injections in my lumbar spine, but none of them helped the pain.

At the VA hospital I had nurses who were nice and that took very good care of me. However, I also had nurses that would roll me over while I was in excruciating pain and pop needles in my hips and arms and tell me, "If you're going to get a high you're going to have to hurt for it."

After 28 days, the doctors released me, still saying they couldn't find anything wrong. They sent me home with the following drugs: Lortab, methocarbamol, Neurontin, promethazine, Effexor, and Demerol. These were powerful, addictive, psychotropic drugs. Heather and I were in the ride of our life and the enemy was trying to take me out, along with trying to destroy our family.

We paid thousands of dollars out of pocket to see doctor after doctor because my condition was getting worse and worse. I could barely stand or walk. I was losing the ability to use my hands and my arms and I could not hold my bladder or bowels. I was also having excruciating pain in my abdomen that kept me from standing up straight and often took me to the floor with pain.

Sometimes we just had to laugh in spite of it all. One day, when Micah was three and very talkative, we were driving back home from Houston and Micah said, "Mama, pull the truck over."

Heather asked, "Why does Mama need to pull the truck over?"

Micah answered, "You have to change Daddy's diaper. He messed his britches again."

Without realizing it, my bowels had moved, a habit that was becoming very embarrassing. But this time we got a good laugh out of it.

I was constantly in and out of the hospital that year. I was also constantly being stuck like a pin cushion by doctors who kept running test after test on me. On top of that I caught MRSA (staff) in one of my hospital stays and it surfaced under both arms and on my face. This was excruciating painful and nasty to boot. The doctors were unable to make it numb when they had to lance and clean out all of the areas. Heather had to pack and clean out the wounds twice a day for several weeks as they healed from the inside out.

It was the middle of May 2010 and the VA had done nothing, so we started relying on my Medicare to get something done. Our marriage as well as my health was deteriorating at hyper speed.

We went to see a chiropractor in Houston, Dr. Robert Lambeth. He examined me and ran some nerve studies. He said, "I could say come here two or three times a week and let me do treatments on you and I will get you feeling better; however, you have some serious damage that needs to be dealt with, and dealt with now, or you won't be walking."

Dr. Lambeth is a man of integrity and honor and a man of God. He got me an appointment with a spine specialist in North Houston in fewer than three weeks. We went to see Dr. S in July 2010, expecting to have some tests run and to have to come back again to see the results. To our surprise, Dr. S said, "I'm sending you straight to the hospital. You will have surgery tomorrow." Wow!

So, God sent us to Dr. Lambeth, and Dr. Lambeth sent us to Dr. S, and Dr. S is the one who started repairing me. Dr. Lambeth is more than just a doctor to me to this day. God is so good even when we don't see His resolve. He is so faithful even when we don't hear His voice.

Heather and I were once again excited and optimistic. It was like the pressure buildup had been released. I had the surgery. Dr. S. had to go into the front and remove all the hardware except for the rods in the back.

The VA kept telling me nothing was wrong. Dr. P and Dr. W kept telling me nothing was wrong. In fact, Dr. P told me that there was nothing I could do to break or damage anything he had done. What we discovered was that the cage he had placed around my spine was the improper cage. It was also the wrong size, and it had broken loose because it was placed wrong. On top of that, over 80% of the damaged and dead disc had been left in my spine at L5 S1. Dr. S repaired all of this. I was in the hospital for a week, but I walked out on my own two feet.

Dr. S prescribed me Norco, promethazine and Soma for pain control. He knew that my neck needed to be dealt with, but that would have to wait after having this major surgery done to repair my lumbar spine properly. What Dr. S did not know that Soma was my Goliath. And when Soma and Norco were combined, it was like kryptonite to Superman. It was very destructive to me and my family.

Here I had faced this giant and walked away without a limp because of God's goodness. Our family should've been grateful and excited about this victory, yet once again, even after God parted the Red Sea, I looked back to Egypt instead of looking at Him for direction.

CHAPTER 27

# MEDICATIONS AS MY GOD

We had to stay with my mother-in-law for almost three weeks until Dr. S released me to make the drive home to Henderson. We were in total turmoil while staying at Heather's mom's. It was my fault, and I didn't even realize what I was doing because I was so blinded by the medications that I was taking. As usual, I was able to justify it because of my neck damage and because I had just had my lumbar spine rebuilt. My disobedience was damaging my family just as my father's had done to my mom and siblings.

Here I called myself a Christ follower, yet I was following the god of medications and using every excuse to do so. I had many convinced that I was in tremendous pain and that I had no other way out, but I refused to listen to my wife and try something different. I had been programmed to self-destruct once again and it was destroying my marriage.

Our pastor at the time came over to counsel us. His advice was to separate for a while. He even told us that we just needed to get a divorce, but we knew that is not what God wanted us to do. I went to my brother Dewayne's house for almost three weeks. He and my sister-in-law Becky were extremely support-ive.

I came back home to find that my wife and son had moved down to my mother-in-law's house in Sugar Land. Boy, was the battle on. While she was gone, I made a lot of poor choices out of anger and due to the impairment from the medications.

But then we started getting along again. I would go down to Sugar Land and spend time with her and Micah. We knew that we loved each other and that we wanted to honor God, but something had to change. It had to start with our walk with God.

Heather and Micah moved back up to Henderson. We need-ed a church like The Bridge Fellowship in Sugar Land, a church that preached God's Word and was loving and faithful to pray. We called up a dear friend of ours, Todd McGrew, and asked him if we would like Mobberly Baptist Church in Longview. He had grown up in that church and he said without hesita-tion, "You'll love it!" We started going to Mobberly immediate-ly. It was the place where we were supposed to be.

In September I went to see Dr. S. Even though he is a very competent neck surgeon, he recommended that I see someone who had even more expertise in the severe damage that I had. I was completely losing the use of my left hand and arm and even my right arm and swallowing was getting to be very diffi-cult. I had tremendous pain traveling down both of my sides. I was having blurred vision and horrible headaches and my anx-iety began to increase. I thought that taking more medications would help, but without my knowing it they were actually in-creasing my anxiety and pain.

Dr. S sent me to Dr. Amir S. Malik in Houston, who exam-ined me. He said my fusions had collapsed and that my neck had collapsed because Dr. P had put in the wrong hardware, and that what he had put in he had placed improperly. He said that I needed my neck operated on as soon as possible, but since I had just had a very difficult surgery done on my lumbar spine, I needed to wait at least six months. We agreed, however, to do it in four, in November. Heather and I got back together in September of 2010 and my surgery was on November 15, 2010.

November finally arrived. We left our home that was torn apart from remodeling. We were discouraged over the lack of progress on our home as well as my health, but now at least we had hope once again about my health. We were also thankful that I had outside insurance to get my issue corrected before it caused permanent damage. We had begged the VA to help us, but they refused to acknowledge that there was serious damage in my neck, just like they did with my lumbar spine. The VA hospital refused to help us in any way, even though we had all of the proof, reports, films and statements from Dr. Malik, a prominent board-certified neurosurgeon. Our small group from church (the LaJoie class) had special prayer for me before my neck surgery. They were faithful to keep praying and check on us more than once a day.

The surgery lasted over nine hours. When I woke up I was very medicated and I had a huge brace on my neck. I remember Micah feeding me ice and saying, "Daddy, I love you." My wonderful wife, Heather, was right there by my side.

The damage was more than the doctor expected, but thank God that Dr. Malik was well prepared to handle any situation that was put before him. He checked on me every day at my bedside; I was not used to this kind of doctor at all. I actually had a doctor who truly cared and was very patient with me.

We went to my mother-in-law's home and stayed there a month and a half until I was able to travel. I was doing really well for the first several days until I ran out of the Soma. The medications started wearing off in my muscles and the areas that were repaired.

One morning I woke up and was having breathing and swallowing problems brought on by anxiety and muscle tension. I felt like I couldn't breathe. The back of my throat and tongue were numb because of the severed nerves from the surgery.

We got me back in to see Dr. Malik. He said the PTSD from the traumatic injury and the war had flared up again. He gave me medication to calm it down. He had already started detoxing me off of pain medications. He told me that in two or three months he would have to put rods from my thoracic spine up to C3 to brace my neck. Then I would be able to go without the neck brace.

The anxiety continued to get worse. The anxiety caused tension and the tension caused pain and the pain caused more anxiety. This is a vicious cycle that anxiety creates in the body and it causes all of your senses to overreact, which causes even more anxiety.

I couldn't get food down and I could barely get water down. I realize now that the muscles were healing and that the nerves were starting to fire again. At the same time all of the medications that I had been on were causing psychosis and even a kind of schizophrenia brought on by the strong narcotics and mind-altering drugs that I had been prescribed over time. My inability to concentrate or reason, as well as irrational fears, were driving me, my wife and my mother-in-law crazy. Even Dr. Malik felt discouraged by it all.

## CHAPTER 28

# TURNAROUND

Because of the serious anxiety that I was going through, Dr. Malik decided to go ahead and operate on the back of my neck to protect any hardware from shifting. To give you an idea of how much hardware it took to repair me, my neck is 98% titanium now. We set the second surgery for November 30. It was a difficult procedure and I was anxious about it. Dr. Malik would be going through the back of my neck and placing rods from my thoracic to the base of C3 in my cervical spine to hold my neck in place and protect where he had to remove a few vertebrae. Heather prayed with me and encouraged me as I waited in the hospital prep room.

While I was waiting in my little cubicle for surgery, I was silently praying for peace and for God to help me through this. I felt all alone and fearful, when suddenly I felt a peace that could only come from God. God spoke to my heart as strongly as He had done many times in the past. He told me that it was all going to be OK. The surgery lasted eight hours. When I woke up Dr. Malik was standing there. He said, "Look, man, you don't have a brace on anymore!"

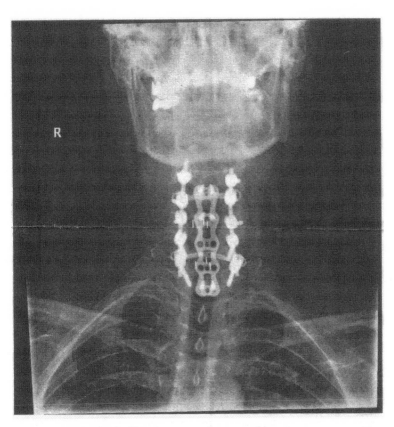

Front x-ray of my neck.

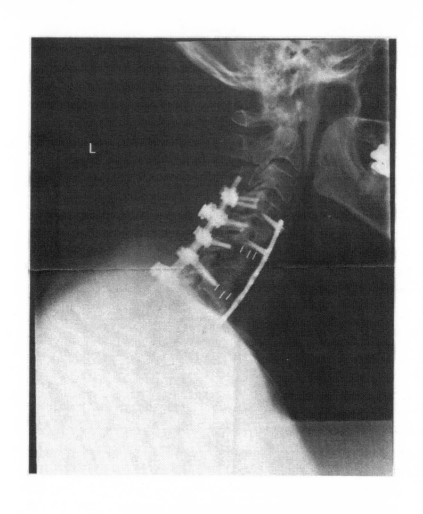

Side x-ray of my neck.

When they removed the drain tube from my neck, the pressure felt like it was choking me and restricting my ability to swallow. This was all part of the healing process, but the effects of narcotic addiction were causing double the anxiety from the repairs. My body had to start absorbing the fluids from the wound and my inflammation response and my body's immune system had to start up once again. The medications that I had been on for many months had suppressed my immune system as well as my body's natural ability to produce gaba, the endorphins that create a natural calm and relaxation as well as being a natural painkiller for the body.

My brain had to be detoxed and fed good nutrition as well as learning to function without synthetic narcotics once again. The body and brain take time to heal and it must be fed consistently with the proper nutrition and exercise. I learned from Dr. Lambeth that the brain can only focus on one big thing at a time and I had to learn to get past the anxiety and start focusing on something other than my injury.

We were at Grandma and Granddad Miller's house until almost February of 2011, and then Dr. Malik released us to go home to northeast Texas. I was detoxed off of the pain medications for several months. These were crucial times for my healing process.

Dr. Kecman in Henderson gave me an equation for anxiety and, man, does it make sense. Muscles without movement equals anxiety. I have found this to be a true statement, whether injured or not.

When we got back to Henderson we were exhausted and worn out because of all of the surgeries, treatment and the anxiety that I was dealing with. My family dealt with the anxiety just like I did, because I am part of their lives also. I was a basket case and my nerves were on edge at all times. I lived in fear in a huge way. I would not go to sleep because I feared I would quit breathing. I feared going outside and walking because I was afraid I would have a panic attack and not make it home. I was becoming a hermit and my anxiety was becoming debilitating. I would, however, go to church. Being involved in church activities kept me sane.

To our surprise, we had a huge Christmas when we got back home. The LaJoie class had all pitched in and bought us all Christmas gifts. They didn't even know we had gone without for the Christmas season, and they helped us out financially without knowing that we were struggling because of all the medical bills. But God knew and He stepped in and worked through His people. Heather and I attended a marriage seminar by Gary Smalley and Ted Cunningham which was powerful and timely. We also attended Dave Ramsey's Financial Peace University, which helped us tremendously.

One night I was very discouraged about all of the anxiety. I got a phone call from a man named Chris who was in our small group from church. Chris said that he and his family were praying for me to be able to swallow again, and for me and my family to start healing. That touched me in a mighty way. God reminded me once again that it was going to all be OK.

The next morning during my quiet time I wrote in my journal about God's faithfulness and how He tells us to not fear. The acronym FEAR stands for False Evidence Appearing Real. I had heard this years before, but it took many years for it to start to resonate in my mind and heart.

After I was done with my quiet time, Heather told me to go to Whataburger and get us all breakfast. I hesitated. I was still afraid of leaving the house because of panic attacks. Heather said, "Curtis, you are going to have to get past this. You need to go and go by yourself."

So I drove for the first time in months. I got our breakfast, but I didn't eat any on the way home. I never, ever took a bite those days without having something to wash it down with quickly. But as I was driving home it was like God stepped into our truck and said, "Curtis, take a bite of that hamburger." I hesitated and looked around my seat. But I had nothing to drink. So because of fear I didn't do it. God spoke to my heart in a strong way once again, saying, "Curtis, take a bite of that hamburger; it's going to be OK."

I remembered Chris calling the night before and praying. I also knew that my wife had faith in God and in my ability to overcome these fears because she made me go. I took a bite of hamburger and I swallowed without any problem. It was God. I was starting to overcome my fears. I knew everything was going to be OK, just as God had told me. Was this the end of the anxiety? No, but it was the beginning of the healing inside. It was the start of my journey to trust God in a deeper way.

After fighting with the VA to pay for my physical therapy, I finally got it approved. I started doing physical therapy at CORE in Longview, Texas under Dr. David Penn. I started learning about the surgery's effects on my muscles and tendons. What I was going through with my swallowing was normal. I knew that I was lucky to be walking and using my arms and hands again and that I was pain free. Through time and consistent therapy, I was learning to overcome my anxiety and learning to use my arms and legs effectively once again.

I was introduced to Anthony Ogden, a personal trainer who put me on the "Super Slow" program. This program focused on strengthening my muscles while building endurance. I had the use of my muscles again; now it was time to get them strong and in shape. Anthony was both patient and stern. He motivated me to do things I thought I would never do again. Gradually, I started to feel like myself once more. My physical therapy allowance from the VA ran out, so I had to stop. Dr. Malik had told me that my life would be one of maintaining my health through exercise, diet, and nutrition, and I was completely committed to that. I was functioning very well and I had been off pain medications for over a year. Heather and I were doing great and God provided us the means to be able to finish our home. It was even picked to be on the Tour of Homes in Henderson! Heather did such an awesome job of designing our home and decorating it that everyone who walked in said that they felt like they were in a magazine because it was so beautiful.

We were honored to be able to go on a mission trip to help with a church plant in Preston, England that our church, Mobberly Baptist, had helped start. God provided every dime for us to go and even provided an excess amount, so we were able to help someone else go over to England and serve.

I was speaking at a Celebrate Recovery meeting at Mobberly. God provided the opportunity to share with a guy named Kevin about obedience, which God significantly used in his life. Kevin became a close friend. Later, I was honored and blessed to do the wedding ceremony for Kevin and his wife Rhonda, which was held at our house. God continued to open up doors to be able to serve Him.

We were also able to take a two-week trip to Florida like we had always wanted to do as a family, visiting Disney, Bush Gardens, Sea World, and the beaches.

Back home, we purchased the property next door to us in hopes of being able to move into it and make a bed and breakfast out of our big house. If we moved next door, I wouldn't have to go up and down the stairs anymore, which was difficult. Pretty soon, we could move into the new home. For the first time in a long time, everything was looking up.

## CHAPTER 29

# CHAOS

Thread by thread, everything started unraveling. First the bed and breakfast didn't work out. The town didn't give us a permit, which was disappointing, especially since we now owned both properties. One day I went to Dallas in our truck, pulling a trailer, to pick up some furniture for our house. Unfortunately, someone had parked in the traffic lane and I was unable to dodge them. I hit the car hard and damaged our truck pretty badly. Thank God it was still drivable. I was able to get the furniture and return home to Henderson.

A few days later, though, I realized that my left leg was going numb and I had a shooting pain down to my foot. My bowels were also losing continence again. Once again, Heather and I thought, *Oh, no, here we go.* We had been on the mountaintop and many encouraging things were happening and it was so obvious that God was moving on our behalf and then this happened.

We went to Good Shepherd Hospital in Longview and they put me in a room and started pain medications to control the severe pain I was having. They did an MRI and we waited a long time for the results.

I was blessed to have a good friend, Gary Hanson, from our small group at church as a nurse at Good Shepherd. Gary was there when the doctor walked in with the MRI results. I knew something was wrong. Gary came over and put his hand on my shoulder. I started shedding tears because I knew what was wrong. The impact from the wreck had driven scar tissue down between the rods in the back of my spine and it was swelling and compressing my spinal cord. It would only get worse without surgery.

I called Heather and told her they were sending me by ambulance to Houston to get this fixed before it caused irreversible damage. We decided that she and Micah would come down the next morning. The surgery was longer than expected, but Dr. S said it went fine.

I got out of the hospital a few days later and we were able to drive home. Unfortunately, the surgery led to a host of problems. I was once again on medications and, once again, I got addicted. I tried going to physical therapy again, but the pain was still excruciating and I had hardly any use of my left leg. My left foot was practically dead and would not move. Dr. S ran several tests and so did the VA. They said that levels L3 and L4 were damaged according to the nerve studies, but the MRI and CT milo-gram did not show any compression. This meant that there was permanent nerve damage. Dr. S wanted me to have a spinal cord stimulator put in my spine.

I started struggling with anxiety again and like a dummy I still didn't tie it to the medications I was taking. I started to gain a lot of weight, jumping from 175 pounds to 268 in less than a year.

In April 2013 I was moving Gary Hanson's trailer from our driveway at the big house to the driveway of our property next door. Heather was out there to help stop traffic so I could do it. I was waiting to turn, with my turn signal on, when a lady hit the trailer that was hooked to my truck going 45 miles per hour without ever braking her vehicle. Everything went black and I lost consciousness. Heather saw the whole thing. Our past flashed before her eyes and she was heartbroken. I was taken to Good Shepherd by ambulance. On the way I started to wake up. Boy, did I hurt. I said to the ambulance driver, "Don't manipulate my neck."

"Why?" he asked.

"Because it's almost all titanium."

I could tell he didn't believe me. As they started doing a CT scan at the hospital, he jokingly commented to the technician, "This guy claims his neck is all titanium." The technician looked at the scan and said, "His neck is almost all titanium." I could tell the ambulance guy felt bad for doubting me.

One encouraging thing was seeing my friend Shawn Smith, Jr. and pastor Greg Martin waiting for me in the room they put me in. Shawn told the nurse that he knew I was in pain because I wasn't talking. I do have a bit of a motor mouth. Heather sometimes tells people to run while she takes my batteries out.

They finally got the pain under control, but it kept me quiet the rest of that day. So did the worry of what was next. I was supposed to start doing some supervising work for a man at church the next day. That would have to wait.

I saw Dr. S in Houston a few days later to make sure everything was OK. He ran some tests and found that I was having severe weakness on my left side, even paralysis on the left side of my face. Fearing I was having a brain bleed or stroke, Dr. S called an ambulance to take me to the hospital.

I was in the hospital for several days and they ran a plethora of tests on me, but found nothing out of the ordinary. They thought I just had nerve damage and finally sent me home. I went to work for the man at church and did some mechanic work as well as supervising. Heather got pretty upset at me doing physical work. I was on pain medications, which contributed to me making poor decisions. And I kept reaggravating my injuries, which caused me to take more pain medications.

Our marriage started falling apart again. There was a lot of anger in our home, and it started feeling like a war zone. God had set me free and now for some reason I had taken my eyes off of Him again and I was depending on the pain medications. The whole time Heather was trying to get me to try natural ways of pain management, but I refused. I kept telling her, "Honey, you don't understand the pain that I am in and you never will." Sadly, I didn't understand the pain that she was in and the pain that our son Micah was in.

## CHAPTER 30

# SEPARATION

I was going to several doctors at this time to try to get the pain and anxiety under control. I couldn't focus on anything, and I started letting the bills go unpaid. Then for some reason I was let go from my job. I didn't even know why. The church offered us counseling, but I had everybody convinced that I needed these medications and I could justify it because of my injuries. I was blinded and the counseling didn't go like we had hoped. (I came to see later that our counselor, Tony Puckett, was actually great at what he did.)

In December 2014 I was admitted into the VA hospital for pain management and tests. They put me on stronger pain medications, a huge mistake. Heather picked me up from the hospital in Shreveport. She was a very unhappy camper, but I still started griping on our way home. She drove me to Longview, where my car was still parked. Despite car trouble, I made it home to Henderson.

I got to our home and Heather, Micah and Duke, our Great Dane, were nowhere to be found. Boy, was I even angrier now. I started having thoughts that Heather hated me and she wanted to divorce me and take everything that I had and even keep me from our son whom I loved dearly. My addiction was starting to really destroy my life—and theirs.

I didn't understand, of course, why she had left. What had started out so wonderfully years before with our marriage had turned into a nightmare. Heather wanted to honor God with her thoughts and her attitudes and her actions, but she had found herself slipping from kindness and empathy into anger and then bitterness. She knew that that wasn't the kind of person she wanted to be.

She and Micah went down to Sugar Land, near Houston, to stay with her mother. She wanted to get away and clear her mind and simply pray. She told me later, "I got on my face and started crying out and saying to God, 'I need You to change this situation, because I can't do anything about it.' I prayed and prayed and prayed and I started to see God change my heart."

I was still seeing Tony, our counselor, on my own. Heather took Micah out of East Texas Christian School in Kilgore, a place he loved. I was blaming everything on her. Early in our marriage, Heather had made a few comments to me that proved to be so true. She said, "Hurt people hurt people." She also said, "Submission comes easy when you know that the one that you are submitting to has your best interest at heart." But now she had no reason to think that I had her best interest at heart. I had my best interest at heart and was simply escaping reality with my medications.

I truly thought that the medications were the only way to deal with the mental, physical and emotional pain that I was in. God had not left me, but He wasn't going to allow me to be comfortable in the choices I was making. I truly felt that I was the one in the right. I ridiculed Heather and told everyone my side of the story without her being able to defend herself.

I wasn't able to be with my family for Christmas and I grew even angrier. I bought another car because I was stranded. That began a vicious cycle of poor financial decisions that affect us to this day. As if buying the car wasn't a bad enough decision, I decided it wasn't a good enough car for me. I traded it in and bought another one. Then I got a credit card with a high credit amount. I was buying things for everybody at this point. I was trying to buy the store for our son, hoping he would love Daddy more for it.

Down in Sugar Land, Micah was admitted into a great Christian school. Because I was not thinking straight I messed that up for him without even meaning to—all because I was mad at Heather for being a mother to him. The drugs were destroying me and us and everything we had.

I made more poor choices by bringing people into our home in the name of helping them. I had no discernment to determine that they were literally robbing me before my eyes. I had charged up several credit cards and I was still waiting and praying for our home to sell before I lost it.

Then I filed for divorce. From my warped point of view, I didn't have any choice. I felt like Heather didn't want me to see our son. In reality, she was just trying to protect him from harm.

I had had my second new car for about two months when, on the way to getting more medications at the VA in Shreveport, I was in an accident in Longview. I kept on driving to get my medications, even with a wrecked car with the air bag out.

A few weeks later, I was driving a rental car, going to my sister's in Oklahoma with Micah. I got into another wreck. It blew the air bags and totaled the rental car and bruised up Micah. God was trying to get my attention again, but I was too blinded by the medications to realize it. I am so thankful that He continued to protect Micah and me. He was simply answering Heather's prayers. While I was messing up all of our lives, she was praying. I am so thankful for a praying wife and Micah is so blessed to have such a faithful, praying mother.

I didn't have any excuse for the financial disaster that I was creating. I had taken the Dave Ramsey class on financial peace. I learned biblical principles of finance. I had applied them until I chose to depend on the medications instead of God.

I was so distraught and angry that I kept purchasing material things to try to make myself happy. But none of the things I bought brought me happiness. People were using me in every way that they could and I was too blinded to see it. The financial hole I was digging was getting deeper and deeper. If you had asked me, I would have said I was honoring God, that I was making wise decisions, and that Heather was my arch enemy. I had other people convinced as well that she was the enemy and that she was at fault for everything. Of course, I was the one who was delusional and confused. I had failed to come to my senses and admit my addictions. Medications and material things had become my gods, and they were destroying me.

We finally got a contract on the big home. It was due to close on February 1, 2016. I was paying Heather child support because I had filed for divorce in March 2015 out of anger and revenge.

I look back in sadness at the person I had become at this point. Here I was, a minister of the gospel, making very ungodly choices. I felt very convicted for who I had become, but I didn't know who to turn to. I wanted to come clean, but I feared the repercussions of doing so. I kept covering up even more by taking more medications.

I hired a man and his wife to do some work on the big house

so that it would pass inspection. I even allowed them to live on the property next door for free after the house had closed and I had received my portion of the sale. I started doing things to the home on impulse. Even though I had paid off my credit cards, I had them all maxed out again in no time.

I was buying stuff for the couple that seemed to be helping me, but they were actually taking advantage of me and eventually robbed me blind. They charged me $3000 to do the electrical wiring on the house after lying to me and the city inspector about their ability to do it. Eventually I had to pay to get the whole thing redone. Their actions broke my heart because I truly cared for them and wanted to help them. I was so blinded that I thought they cared about me and that they were helping me. I was reaping what I had sown and the sad thing is that my bad choices deeply hurt my whole family.

On January 4, 2016, Micah and I were in a car wreck in Houston. My car was totaled and it terrified me that Micah had gotten hurt, but thank God he ended up OK. The wreck was not my fault like the previous ones had been, but the damage was done. The accident really hurt my spine and neck and tore up my left shoulder. I got a new car, but I had to sell it because I couldn't afford the insurance. When I sold it, I wasn't even wise with the money from the sale. Because of all the strong medications, I just couldn't think straight.

When, I wondered, would all of this finally end?

CHAPTER 31

# Restored

In March 2016 God started to break through the fog in my mind. I had been sincerely praying again. The divorce was due to be final at the end of March. In His sovereignty, God pushed back the finalization more than once. I was getting angry at my attorney, but now I see that it was God's hand. I started reading my Bible again and truly seeking God.

The VA was taking me off of the medications and they wanted me to go through detox at the VA hospital, but they wanted to switch me over to Methadone, a synthetic heroine. I had been on that stuff before and I was not about to go on it again.

Micah, my nephew Cayden, and I went to San Antonio for four days and had a really good time in the city and at Six Flags Over Fiesta Texas.

We came home and I knew in my heart that there had to be a change and it needed to be now. I feared the Methadone and the VA system, so I called around and found a detox program at ETMC Tyler Behavioral Unit. The night before I went into rehab, I told Micah that he was going to have to go back to Momma's place early because Daddy had something to do. He got very angry at first because he wanted to spend the whole time with me. But then I told him that I was going to detox.

Micah hugged me tight and, with tears running down his cheeks, he said these precious words to me: "I told you, Daddy, that Jesus was going to put you and Momma back together. I told you so!"

I was not sure of my future, but I was sure that God was leading me once again. Even if I didn't recover my family, I would get my life back and my relationship right with God once again. I went to battle and the battle was the detox. On my way there, Heather suggested we put off the divorce. She also told me how proud of me she was.

God knew that I needed to hear these words from her and He knew that she had never ceased praying for me. She had never wanted the divorce. I had believed that she was my enemy, but that was a lie from our true enemy.

I checked myself into rehab on Palm Sunday weekend. I expected to stay a while, but I was ready and I knew that God was with me. Heather kept leaving messages of encouragement for me. God knew that would help me keep going. God was so good to surround me with Christian nurses, which was also a tremendous help for me. God even used me to share the gospel with several people while He had me getting clean.

My eyes and ears were finally open to hear the truth about these narcotics and their effects on the human body and brain. I was devastated to hear what I heard, but I was ready to learn and change. God had sent me into battle armed with His Word and leading me by His Holy Spirit within my heart. I was dealing with a tremendous amount of pain while I was in the facility. My shoulder was hurting badly, as were my hip and leg. I felt God crawl into the bed with me and remind me that it was going to be OK and that He would never leave me. He had changed my heart and opened my eyes to the truth about the medications. I learned that I was having seizures from them and that my liver was in bad shape, causing more pain. I learned the side effects of all of the drugs that I was on. It was sickening and eye-opening to see who these drugs had made me.

When I got home, Micah and I went fishing in Galveston. The next day we went to Sugar Creek Baptist Church and watched Heather sing in the choir on Easter Sunday. God had not just resurrected my life, but He also resurrected our marriage.

This is what our God wants to do for us on a daily basis: give us hope and purpose and resurrect us from the pains and damage of sin. He wants to free us with His awesome grace, mercy and forgiveness.

As my mind got clearer, the couple that was living on our property and did me so wrong were not able to get away with what that had gotten away with for months. They moved on. I counted my losses and Heather simply asked me if I had learned from this. I had, and, boy, was it a painful lesson.

At this point, shortly after I had returned from detox, Heather was hopeful about us, but she honestly didn't know how long it might last. We spent more and more time together, however, as I learned to court my wife once again. I was blessed and honored to have my wife back and I am so grateful to God for His intervening. Micah and I did all the work that we could to our remaining home in Henderson. We were all together in Sugar Land in August. By that time, six months after my detox, Heather knew that God had truly answered her prayers. He had already changed her heart. Now my life had changed, and so had our family's.

Heather had to bail me out of many financial binds, but she did so with love and compassion and not judgment. We were learning to love and trust each other again, even in the midst of the past being thrown up in our faces daily. We faced even more hardship when the state pulled my driver's license for health reasons. They said I could reapply for one in a year. Heather and I had seen God move on our behalf so much by this time. Our marriage being restored was a huge miracle.

We asked for prayer on my behalf about my driver's license. We took the driver's license issue to court. I told a good friend that I was going to praise God no matter the outcome. I was learning to praise God in the storm once again. We were already figuring out how we were going to make it work, living in Sugar Land and me not having a license. A week later I called to see if the Texas Medical Review Board had received letters from several doctors who did physicals on me and stood up for me on my behalf. The lady on the phone said, "Mister Brown, are you sitting down?" I said, "Yes ma'am, why do you ask?" She said, "I have never seen this before, but you got your driver's license back." What an awesome God we serve! God had parted the Red Sea for me once again.

I started acupuncture and medical massage therapy when I got out of rehab, which has continued to this day. The VA approved and started paying for my natural treatments, which helped my PTSD and pain. I was able to work out regularly, which both helped my pain and my weight, which dropped from 270 to 205. I began feeling better than I had in years.

We finished the work on our home in Henderson and it sold. We bought a home in Richmond, Texas, right next to Sugar Land. I started substitute teaching at Fort Bend Christian Academy, an incredible blessing. We are debt free except for our home mortgage. Micah is doing great and I am so proud of him. We are all thriving together at Sugar Creek Baptist Church.

God is moving in so many ways and using us once again. I am very careful to not let my guard down on the battlefield again. The mines are hidden out there, but God is my commander and He knows where they all are. When I keep my eyes on Him, He guides me around them.

God reminded me while I was in detox that I was like Peter. I stepped out onto the water, but when the storms came I focused on the waves and I took my eyes off of Him. He held me above water just enough to keep me from drowning.

I was blessed on Labor Day weekend in 2016 to do the wedding ceremony of my old neighbor near Fort Hood, Texas, Rich Rogers. Rich and I had become close friends during a painful time in both of our lives. We had served together in Iraq. Rich was an Apache pilot and instructor and he just happened to be my air support in the Persian Gulf War. Both of us had tried to take our lives because of the pains of war. But God had other plans for each of us, and He brought incredible healing to both of us. He can do it for anyone who trusts Him and surrenders their life to Him.

CHAPTER 32

# WHERE I'VE BEEN, AND WHERE I'M HEADING

If someone asked me where I had been and the direction I was heading, here's what I would tell them.

I am a Persian Gulf War veteran who was medically retired from injuries sustained during my service in the US Army. I enlisted in the United States Army in 1989 and served for a total of eight years as a heavy equipment and helicopter mechanic. I was a lead mechanic for our battalion in the Iraqi staging area and at the Port of Jabal in Saudi Arabia. I received 2 Bronze Service Stars, Army Achievement Medal, Coin of Excellence, Expert Marksman, Mechanics Badge, Grenade Badge, and Combat Medic Badge. I was medically retired in 1998.

I have had 19 surgeries, along with nearly losing my life from the effects of military injuries, PTSD, chemical exposure, and addiction to narcotics and psychotropic meds that the VA had given me over the course of 18 years. I was told that I would never be able to function without these medications for the remainder of my life.

My surgeries have included five on my left knee, four on my lumbar spine, four on my cervical spine, two on my shoulders, appendix and gall bladder removals, and abdominal exploratory surgeries. My lumbar spine is held together by rods and screws and my neck is now 98% titanium.

I started a journey of trying to find something to help my chronic pain, PTSD/anxiety and addiction. I was less than a month out from finalizing my divorce. Yet God never gave up on me, nor did my wife and son. They, along with many others, faithfully prayed and waited until God stepped in and provided us the long-awaited answer we had been searching for. I was sick of the medications that were controlling my life, but not controlling the pain/anxiety. I learned that they were causing my body more pain and anxiety because my body was not designed to break down all of the synthetics that are in the medications.

On March 17, 2016 I checked myself into a hospital for three days so they could monitor me as I detoxed off all of my medications. The very day that I got out, I went to a local chiropractor and started using Eastern medicine such as acupuncture, medical massage therapy, and natural oils for healing and pain management. Little did I know that these would help the PTSD and anxiety as well. I have been pain free, PTSD/anxiety free, as well as medication free since March 18th, 2016. Being pain free has allowed me to do things I could have never done in the past, such as work out at a local gym and interact normally with my family once again.

In the next year and a half, I lost over 80 pounds and I felt better than I had in years. My transformation was truly a heart issue. Once I let go of my fears and determined to obey God and not allow addiction to control my life any longer, He stepped in and gave me wisdom and direction. He healed my mind and body and restored my family.

I continue to be on a strong regimen of exercise, acupuncture, diet, proper supplements, and massage therapy. All of these have been an integral part of my recovery. I do strengthening exercises two times a week and exercise my shoulders, back, triceps and lumbar spine at least three times a week. I use the treadmill for cardio to burn more energy, which in turn burns the anxiety, helps move the toxins out of my muscles, and helps get more oxygen to my brain. This increase in oxygen is a huge part of controlling PTSD and anxiety because it burns up cortisol and helps the mind relax.

The entire regiment of exercise is key to being able to relax and heal. I swim one day a week, and I use the hot tub to relax my muscles even more which helps me to stretch them more effectively.

Over the years I explored many avenues to find true peace as well as true freedom. What I found was that we can be imprisoned by the very things that we are told by society will set us free. I found out the hard way that medications, material things, and even sexual fulfillment are not the key to freedom and inner peace. After many years of struggling I eventually realized the true bondage into which these addictions had placed me. I learned that true peace is something that remains constant even when you are in the middle of a battle. The god that I once visualized in the life of my dad was not the one true living God who truly wants to set us free from any prisons we are in.

I finally learned that putting my full trust in Jesus Christ was the only thing that could give me the true peace and freedom that I had been searching for all of my life. And I learned that true victory comes through fully surrendering to God. When God opened my eyes to His truth, I was able to overcome the addictions as well as the mental scars through the love of Jesus Christ.

But we can't do it alone. Being a part of a communal atmosphere of well-being has been vital for my recovery. I encourage everyone to be a part of a Bible teaching church in order to grow spiritually. I was able to overcome my chronic pain, addiction and PTSD/anxiety and depression through the love of Jesus and the encouragement of others.

At the prompting of many people, including my neurosurgeon, Dr. Amir S. Malik of Houston, I started writing this book about my life story. My desire was simply to help others struggling with the same things I struggled with. You could call me a survivor. In addition to all I struggled with, I tried to take my own life in 2000 and 2001, but God spared me for this day and time.

My wife, Heather, our son, Micah, and I, along with our English bulldog, Uga, now have our own home in Richmond, Texas. We continue to worship and grow at Sugar Creek Baptist Church in Sugar Land. God has moved us forward and continues to lead me closer to Him. He has given me a passion for those who suffer from abuse, traumatic injuries, PTSD/anxiety, depression and addiction. My heart is to help those who suffer with these issues overcome them in a natural way. I believe that if our minds and bodies are given the proper environment to improve and even heal, they will.

For a couple of last laughs I will share two stories. Bruce Rudd, a pastor in Lindale, Texas, and his wife Tressa are dear friends of ours. This wonderful couple happened to be at our house, checking in on us, after I had gotten home from my neck surgeries.

Bruce said, "Heather, I figured out how we can cover the funeral costs when Curt goes to be with the Lord."

"How?" Heather asked.

Bruce answered, "I can do the ceremony. We can take Curt's body to be cremated and recover all the titanium in his body and sell it. It'll not only pay for the funeral; we'll even have some extra cash from it." God, please let me look down and watch these crazy people try to do this.

Not long after, my dear friend Michael Hunt said to me, "I want to be under you for just a few seconds during the rapture."

"Why would you possibly want that?" I asked him.

"So I can watch all the titanium fall from the sky."

God, this is your story. I pray that You will be honored and that many will come to know You for the first time or in a deeper way through the words of this book. I love you, Jesus, and I am so honored to call you my Savior, my friend and my redeemer.

*PART TWO*

# LESSONS

As my pastor Kenny Dean said during my ordination: "God took a mess of Curtis's life and gave him a message." If I were to summarize it, that message would be this: freedom through forgiveness. That is really what this book, and my life's story, is all about.

Is seems like most of us have to go through the what-it-isn't to finally get to the what-it-is. I did. I finally discovered that what true life is, is Jesus.

Along that path we have a lot of life experiences. If we let them, God will have many things to teach us through those experiences. They build character in us, and it is through these experiences that we become who we are today. Jesus then uses our life's experiences to help others who are struggling with the same heart-wrenching things that we ourselves have gone through and from which have been set free by His love.

I have already told you my life story. In this section of the book, I want to talk about many of the things that, through experiences good and bad, through the laughter and the many tears, God has taught me along the way.

*CHAPTER 33*

# SO THAT'S WHAT THAT
# SHOWS ME!

Looking back on the episodes of my life (many of which I have shared in this book), I see now how so many of them illustrate deep truths about God, ourselves, and life.

I told the story of how, when I was four and we still lived in California, I got lost in the underground tunnels and found myself looking up through the wrong side of a sewage grate. While I was looking up through the bars at freedom, I was afraid and helpless. There was only one tunnel that led me out of the mess I was in, but I couldn't find it myself. My mom had to send my brother to lead me out.

God did the exact same thing for us. We were all trapped in sin, separated from God by a lot more than a sewage grate. We have no way out. And I do mean *no way*. But God loved us, so much more than my mother could have ever loved me (as hard as that is for me to imagine). So, He sent His only Son to this earth to die for us and set us free from sin. He came to get us out the dark and nasty sewage that we were all stuck in.

My mother and my brother didn't wait for me to figure out how to free myself. They knew I was lost and couldn't find my way back. So, they took action themselves to set me free. And was I ever glad to see my brother when he came to rescue me!

One day, when I was still lost and separated from Him, God showed me that Jesus is not waiting for us to get things right in our life before we can come to Him. He knows that He is the only one who can get us out of the situation we are in. We are lost, and we can't get to Him on our own. He has to come to us. He does that when we sincerely cry out to Him to save us. He is coming to us just as we are and wherever we are, if we will call out to Him and place our trust in Him. He never, ever fails to save us.

Around the time I got lost in the tunnels, we had some great Hispanic neighbors who owned a flower shop and a landscaping business. Our mother repeatedly told me and Dewayne to stay away from their flowers and their barrels full of some pretty, bright red things. But Dewayne and I were the most curious of kids. So, one afternoon, we decided to get a closer look at bright red things. We opened the lid of the barrel and started picking the red things up and smelling them and even throwing them at each other. One thing led to another and we started tearing them open. As we got more and more caught up in the fun, we completely forgot about Mom's warning to leave these things alone. It never even dawned on us why she told us that. Maybe it was because she knew that red peppers were in the barrel!

After a while I needed to go pee. So, I went to our back yard and started to go pee, and so did Dewayne. With red pepper juice all over our hands. Guess what happened next? Dewayne and I invented break dancing years before it ever came out. The peppers made our private parts burn so bad that they made us cry. Naturally, we then both started to rub our eyes. Then we started yelling.

Mom heard the commotion and came running outside. When she saw what we had done, she quickly got the water hose to start rinsing us off. Then she put us in the shower. Boy, did those peppers burn! I thought that the burn would never go away and the water didn't seem to help much. Eventually, though, the sting subsided.

Mom reminded us of what she had told us about the red peppers. They were so pretty and tempting, but who would have known the pain that they packed inside of them? Mom knew, and that's why she warned us to leave them alone.

Mom didn't tell us to leave the peppers alone to keep us from having fun. We had lots of ways at our house and in our neighborhood to have fun. She warned us because she knew that they would hurt us. Mom didn't want us hurt because she loved us dearly.

When he was little, I was the same way with my son, Micah. Come to think of it, now that he's twelve, I still am. The ways life can hurt us actually grow more numerous as we get older, and he still needs his father's guidance.

God, of course, is the same way with us. He doesn't tell us to do certain things and to avoid other things because He wants to spoil our fun. Just the opposite! He wants our lives to be as rich and fulfilling as they can possibly be.

But we have all disobeyed God, and suffered the consequences of sin, just like Dewayne and I suffered the consequences of the red peppers. Only, the consequences of sin are much worse. The Bible says that "the wages of sin is death" (Romans

6:23a). Death in this context doesn't just mean physical death. It means eternal separation from God. God is holy, and in our sin we can't spend eternity with a holy God. And there is nothing we can do to make our sin OK. We can't make it go away.

But God created us to be with Him forever, and wants with all of His infinitely great heart for us to be with Him forever, and know His love forever.

So, He sent His Son to rescue us from our sin. Jesus came and died a horrible death on a humiliating cross made for criminals, so that He could remove our bad choices from God's sight. On the cross, Someone who is perfect in every way sacrificed Himself for our sin. He took God's punishment for sin, so that we would not have to.

As a result, "the wages of sin is death, *but the free gift of God is eternal life in Christ Jesus our Lord*" (Romans 6:23, NASB, italics added). Eternal life is a gift. It is not, and never will be, something we can earn by being good enough. It doesn't matter how bad we've been; God's grace through Jesus Christ is always greater. Jesus's sacrifice for our sins is always sufficient.

So how do we receive this free gift? Simply by trusting Jesus and what He did for us.

> But now God has shown us a way to be made right with him without keeping the requirements of the law . . . We are made right with God by placing our faith in Jesus Christ. And this is true for *everyone* who believes, no matter who we are. (Romans 3:21-22, *New Living Translation*, italics added)

As the Apostle Paul wrote, "Thanks be to God for His indescribable gift!" (2 Corinthians 9:15).

It seems as if, around age five, it was always one episode after another with me. Soon after recovering from the red peppers, I was walking barefoot through our carport and I felt a tingle on my feet. The tingle was kind of like a tickle and burn together. I walked across several more times and kept feeling the same tickle/burn. Then, all of a sudden, there was no more tickle and the burn was very, very painful. I started crying, and Mom ran out to me. I told her that something on the carport was burning my feet really bad. She rushed me to the backyard and rinsed my feet with the water hose. As she did, all of the skin started peeling off. Mom called to my dad and asked him what in the world was on the carport. Dad just yelled at me and asked me what I'd been doing there. But Mom turned it right back on him. "They play there every day. What were you doing to cause his feet to get burned?"

As it turned out, Dad had been charging a battery. The battery had gotten hot and started leaking acid all over the concrete. I had been walking through the acid.

Thinking back to the acid that burned my feet, it brings to mind many things I've done in my life that felt good at first but eventually caused a lot of pain. Many times I did things that created a mess just like the acid, and unfortunately, I didn't clean up the mess quickly enough before others were hurt by it.

We can do a lifetime of damage to ourselves and others by making one irrational decision, which is usually led by our emotions and our physical desire for pleasure. Pleasure is not a bad thing if we experience it God's way. As a matter of fact, it is much more enjoyable doing things the way God intended, and it is safe, because it was designed to be safe. What a concept! God did not give us rules to keep us from having fun; He gave us rules for our own protection.

Dad had to cover all of the acid with baking soda to neutralize it, and then he had to wash it all off the carport. It took him quite a bit of time and effort to get the carport clean again.

The Son of God came to clean up the mess that we made in our own lives. He came to clean up our sin. Jesus literally had to cover our sin with His own precious blood in order for it to be rinsed away. Only His blood can remove the reality of eternal separation from God from our lives.

When I was seven I had an experience that felt devastating and humiliating then, but I can laugh about now. My dear cousin Char and her dad, my Uncle Tommy, came to visit us in Oklahoma. Uncle Tommy invited Mom, Dewayne and I go back with them to Phoenix for a few weeks and, boy, were we excited. Uncle Tommy had a truck with a traveling camper on the bed of it. I thought it was cool riding in the camper in the back of a truck. We could talk to Mom and Uncle Tommy through the sliding glass windows in the rear glass of the truck. We didn't have a bathroom in the camper, but we had a pee jar.

Unfortunately, one day the pee jar, full of pee, accidentally fell on my head. Dewayne and Char were always teasing me and playing practical jokes on me, but this time it wasn't their fault. The pee went all over me. I had no place to wash or wipe it off. Mom got mad at Uncle Tommy because he was laughing and refused to pull the truck over, but he finally relented. I was able to clean off and start enjoying the trip again. I even started laughing at what had happened.

Sometimes our lives get in a mess and it's not even our fault or the fault of those around us. These things cover us and make a mess of us, but we need to learn from them. They teach us that life is not always pretty, but we can carry on and enjoy life.

I have learned through this that some humiliating things in our lives can be just to humble us at the time while teaching us to forgive and let it go.

One of my fondest memories before we left California was my cousin Sue's fifth birthday party. At the party all the kids got to ride on a cool Ferris wheel. However, I was terrified to get on it because of my balance issues and not being able to hear much at all. But Sue always encouraged me, even at a very young age, and she did at this time also. She told me I could do it, and helped me on the wheel, and once I was on I enjoyed the ride.

Sometimes, we have to give people a helping hand so that they can feel accomplishment in their lives. We need encourage them to take that first step. It doesn't mean we do it for them. It means we say, "You can do it," and then help them in such a way that they themselves realize they actually can.

Mom always told us to appreciate the little things in life. These little things are special, and God uses them to encourage us as we walk through adversity, such as the constant chaos in my home or even the many challenges that life put before me. My frog-hunting expeditions when I was young were one of those little things in my life that brought me joy in the midst of turmoil.

As I look back at my frog hunting expeditions, I am reminded of a crucial part of the story. When I thought that I was catching the frogs, I was actually setting them free. They had been trapped by the temptation of the food in the water meter boxes.

I remember catching many of the same frogs again and again.

We, too, are often trapped by trying to satiate our appetite with something that looks good but is never fulfilling. And we keep doing it, over and over. Thank you, God, for coming along and getting me out of the traps that I have gotten myself into. Thank you most for sending your Son, Jesus, and setting me free from death and eternal separation from You.

My wife, Heather, summarized it like this: "God sent His Son Jesus to get us out of the water meters (darkness) and then He places us in the light, while giving us eternal life through His Son Jesus Christ." Now, we don't have to live our lives trapped in the water meters, because Jesus gives us the strength to say *no* to the temptation that led us there.

I told the story about how, right after we moved to Oklahoma, I broke through the Red Rover barrier and ran all the way to the Morgans' house because I didn't want to face having to make new friends in a strange place. I didn't want my life to change.

But resisting change is often resisting what God wants for our lives. His plan for us is change: the changes He wants to bring about.

Joyce Morgan did me a huge favor by marching me back to Vacation Bible School and forcing me to face the challenge of change. I eventually learned to make new friends easily. That served me very well in the US Army, where it seemed like change was constant. In making new friends, it helps, I learned, to simply be friendly.

God may want to change your life in a significant way right now. He may want to break you free from chains that have bound you. If you don't know Jesus as your personal Savior, God wants to change your life and help you break through the barriers that are holding you captive. We receive Him as our personal Savior simply by trusting in Him and what He did for us in His death and resurrection.

That faith can be expressed very simply in prayer, which is just talking with God. It can be as simple as this:

> Jesus, I recognize that I need your forgiveness, and the life you offer. Thank you for dying for my sins and rising from the dead on my behalf, so that you could give me true life. I receive you by faith as my Savior and Lord and trust you to forever join me to yourself. Thank you for coming to live within me, and giving me eternal life.

It is not the words of a prayer that are vital. It is the faith that they represent.

Once you have a real relationship with God through Jesus, he will know exactly what you need to do to be set free from the things that have bound you. Sometimes it is people in our lives that we need to break away from—people who have been a bad influence on us. Can that be painful? Yes. But don't be afraid of change; it is always for our own good if it leads us closer to Jesus. I have never once been sorry for being obedient to something God was calling me to do. I have been sorry many, many times for the opposite!

*CHAPTER 34*

# TUNNEL VISION

Have you ever wished that you could live your life with tunnel vision? If we could live our lives with tunnel vision, we would never see the things happening to the left or right of us, and what was behind us would be just that—behind us. We couldn't see what's there unless we literally turned around to see. That sounds appealing at times, doesn't it? Many times in my life, I have wished I could block out what is going on around me or that I could just flip a switch to make the parts of my past that hurt me disappear.

But just because we can't see or hear things doesn't mean they don't affect us.

When I was young, I couldn't hear most of what people around me were saying. And I often didn't turn around to notice what was happening around me, because I didn't hear it. But I was still affected by others' actions. The truth is everything going on around us has an effect on us, just as choices we make affect others as well as ourselves. The question is how we are going to respond to the things that take place in our lives. Do we allow the good things that happen to us override the bad? If I continue to focus only on my past, will it ruin or alter my future?

There are some things that we need to let go of from our past. But there are also some things we need to apply to our lives to prevent us from making a bad choice again. Life's experiences do produce wisdom, if we apply what we have learned to each new situation. We can also learn by listening and applying life lessons from others. Doing these two things can prevent heartache and pain in our lives as well as others' around us. I had a teacher tell me once that, if you stop learning, you stop living. We often learn by listening to those who have good advice to offer from their own life's experiences. This can be a challenge for me. Just ask my wife.

As I was growing up, I made a lot of bad choices while searching for peace and fulfillment. After the war, I was searching even more for peace and happiness in my life. It took me a long time to discover that the starting point of true healing begins by admitting that we are broken and that we must have a deep desire to change.

I was living my life in a tunnel and continuing to travel in one direction while focusing on the world's way of fulfillment, which was continuing to cause so much destruction inside me. After I could go no further, and I had even tried to end my life and failed at that, I realized that I needed a Savior. I needed more than just hearing the stories from the Bible; I needed to take ownership of those stories. That's when God truly stepped into my jacked-up life.

We have to ask ourselves if we are going to allow events in our lives to program our thought patterns. Will we have a continual negative perspective toward our family and others around us? Will our programmed patterns continue to influence our views of our country, or, most important of all, our view of God?

The world around us—the media, the entertainment industry, government, and even religion—always tries to program us to think and act the way it does. Sadly, the world paints a beautiful picture of the very things that bring about destruction. We are deceived into thinking that those things offer freedom and fulfillment. So, we feel free to indulge in things that are mentally, morally and spiritually damaging to the very core of who we were truly created to be. Entire industries exist solely for this purpose.

Much of my life was a history of following these paths. They created a sense of sensual pleasure while giving me a false sense of freedom. I was so caught up in the erotica of it all that I didn't see what was going on around me, behind me or even inside of me. I was given a false peace within, while my whole sense of purpose was being taken away by the path I was choosing to follow. I was living a life of irresponsibility and I wasn't concerned about anything but myself. I was in a tunnel and I had no vision except for desiring anything and everything that would satisfy my sinful desires.

I have discovered that the only One who can give us true inner peace is God, through His Son Jesus Christ. But the things we pursue in the world, that give us false peace, continually separate us from the one thing that can give us true peace and freedom. God truly wants to save us from ourselves as well as the world system. He wants how we think, act, and react to all situations in life to reflect who He truly is, because He knows there is true freedom for us there.

Our society has painted such a distorted picture of God. Most of us can't really say who God is because we don't know Him in a personal way. That's the way I was for years and years. But to know someone, you must first spend time with them.

When we look at our lives, we see many difficult things that have been beyond our control. These may be war, parental abuse, spousal abuse, illness, natural disasters, or a host of other things. How do we look at these things? Do we just condemn those responsible for what has affected our lives? Do we live life for revenge and continually blame God or others for every situation that has affected us?

To find peace, we have to be able to forgive, first, ourselves, and then others. Unforgiveness keeps us stuck in a tunnel while leading us in a constant destructive pattern. But forgiveness is not natural for us without a thriving relationship with Jesus. We find true peace and freedom through true forgiveness, which is supernatural. This takes us out of the tunnel of destruction. People tend to believe that getting even will bring about justification and healing. The reality is that it brings about more destruction, both mentally and spiritually.

I have asked myself many times why I went through the things that I went through, and why I continue to face adversity daily in my life. Some of us want to block out our childhood and other parts of our lives, but the illustration is true: each of our lives is a tapestry. If we blocked out anything, we would not be who we are today.

In any case, we can never truly block out anything in our lives. We can't live with tunnel vision. No matter what we try to do to cover up life's bumps and bruises, it's just a cover-up. It's like having a board in which you hammer several nails. When you remove the nails, the scars from the nails remain. But even though there are scars, this doesn't mean that we can't use the board anymore.

God chooses to use us, scars and all. His only Son died for us so that He could forgive us of all of our sins. It didn't stop there. His only Son Jesus Christ rose up from the dead. You see,

He defeated death! God chooses to use the areas in our lives that left scars to give others hope, and He also chooses to use us to lead others to His Son Jesus.

If we sweep things under the rug of our lives long enough, what we get is a rug with a large mound that both we and others will trip over. Instead, we need to clean things up now. We need to address the issues in our lives head on and take responsibility for our own actions. This process is actually the beginning of healing.

An important first step is admitting where we have been wrong. God tells us to confess our sins. First John 1:9 says, "If we confess our sins, He is faithful and righteous to forgive us our sins and to cleanse us from all unrighteousness" (NASB). Once we know that we have forgiveness from God, we can forgive ourselves. And then we can forgive those who have hurt us, sometimes very deeply.

One of the ironies of my life is that I didn't just become some of the things I hated most in my dad, I became everything I hated and more. I became the very thing I hated because of my own inability to forgive my father, other people, and events in my life that had hurt me. I was hurt from my childhood pain, my wartime pain and from my injuries that used to be a constant reminder of what I went through. The memories of these events in my life kept me locked in the tunnel of destruction. I learned that I cannot forgive on my own.

It took me coming to the end of myself and running out of all my resources (which even meant the medications) before I finally cried out to God. When I was sincere with my cry, He sent His Son Jesus to rescue me where I was. I didn't work on getting myself better so that I could ask for God's help. He came to me right where I was in that sewage tunnel.

Forgiveness requires a change of heart which is supernatural and can only happen by putting our trust in Jesus Christ, asking Him for forgiveness, and asking Him to help us forgive others. The most amazing yet ironic thing is that the tyrant in my life, my dad, eventually became my best friend as well as becoming a Christ follower. He truly did become what Paul described: "Therefore if anyone is in Christ, he is a new creature; the old things passed away; behold, new things have come" (2 Corinthians 5:17, NASB).

We can go many directions in life, just like all of the tunnels that kept leading me in the wrong direction while keeping me in the dark. When, as a young boy, I was lost in the sewage tunnels, there was only one tunnel that would lead me out into the light and to my mother. All of the other tunnels led me farther from my mom while taking me in circles and keeping me in the dark. They were like the tunnels later in my life that misled me, leading me down the wide road that leads to destruction and to eternal separation from God (Matthew 7:13).

I am so thankful that I had a mother who found and rescued me. I am so thankful that I had a God who found and rescued me, too.

## CHAPTER 35

# THE LIGHT OF OUR LIVES

External scars are often a reminder of internal pain. I have had many injuries in my life where the flesh has healed, but internal scars are dealt with daily. Life is a war, a battle between good and evil. Jesus is the lamp and the light, but we have an enemy, and his whole mission is to render us ineffective as Christ followers. Satan will do anything to try to put that light out in our lives or to get us off of the path that Jesus is leading us on. Satan often reminds us of our past and the things that we have done wrong in life; that is why he is called the accuser of the brethren.

We need to focus on the empty tomb. The empty tomb is our reminder that Jesus overcame this world and defeated death. When we put our trust in Jesus as our Savior, we are forgiven of our past mistakes. We have to remember that every time the accuser of the brethren reminds us of our past, God has given us a future with Him through His Son Jesus Christ.

God tells us to renew our minds daily in His Word so that we think as He thinks. God wants us to act and react like Him in any given situation in life. I am reminded of how crucial it is to allow Jesus to be a light unto our path. Psalm 119:105 says, "Your word is a lamp for my feet, and a light on my path." There are so many things that we can't see in this dark world that are lying in wait, ready to cause us harm. This is why we must keep our eyes on Jesus and hide God's Word in our hearts—to protect us from the dangerous things we can't see. But God can see them.

As I was growing up, we all went to the storm cellar because it was a place of protection. But my sister couldn't see the danger that was lying on the floor in her path, the pitchfork. In a place that was supposed to keep us from harm, somebody had tossed the pitchfork down on the floor instead of taking the time to stand it up out of the way.

How often in life do we get lazy and do things half-way and haphazardly? Eventually it can come back to haunt us or even cause pain to someone else. This is why we should always do things as if we are doing them unto the Lord.

Have you ever noticed how dark and creepy and nasty cellars usually are? Cellars were built for our protection, but we don't keep them clean or well lit, so their protection fails us. It reminds me that we need to be diligent not to let dangers lurk. A little diligence in our lives, especially our spiritual lives, goes so far toward protecting us.

Do you ever wonder why the creepiest critters live in the cellar? They live in the dark, just like our enemy Satan. Creepy critters can't stand the light. Neither can Satan. Jesus is the light of the world, and the world can't stand in His presence.

We used to have candles and flashlights in the cellar, but if we didn't have a light going up or down the stairs, getting in and out could be very dangerous. Items lying around, out of place, could be dangerous, too, as Carla found out. It reminds me of how most of us wait until the storm to run to God. We haven't prepared beforehand for the storms by letting Jesus be our light every day. We need "The Light of the World" with us at all times.

Jesus is the storm maker and the storm breaker! God allows storms in our lives to draw us to the one true light, Jesus Christ. But after the storm, He doesn't want us to return to business as usual. There may be deep issues in our hearts that need to be dealt with, and it takes storms to remind us that they are still there and for God to bring them to the surface to make us deal with them.

The cellar is not just for us, and just because it may be our cellar, that doesn't mean that others won't need it for protection. If we have family or friends over and a storm comes, they soon realize if we are prepared for a storm or not. It's the same way in all of life. If we claim to be Christians, storms in our lives will show others where we truly stand with God. These storms affect everyone around us and mostly the ones we love. God wants to clean up our cellars, and He desires to give us a safe place to go during the storms. God sent His only Son Jesus to enter into our cellars, which are our hearts, to clean them up and to give us a peace during the storms in life. When we truly allow Him to clean us up and as we allow Him to be our safe place in the storm, He reveals Himself to all who are around us during the storms. He is the only true peace we (and they) will ever find in the storms of life.

# CHAPTER 36

# OVERCOMING LIFE'S STINGS

When we lived in the old farm house on South Marion Street in Hinton, Oklahoma, I got stung by a bumblebee. I got stung because I was taking a chance by throwing rocks at its hive. I knew that the bumblebees would come after me, and it became a game to me, and I didn't consider the consequences, like getting stung. I knew better than to do what I was doing because Mom and Dad told me that the bees would sting me and that their sting was very painful. I kept on because I had gotten attached to the thrill of danger, and eventually I got stung, and, boy, did it hurt.

I was messing with God's creatures that were designed to protect each other, even to their death. I was hooked on the emotional high, and I got so caught up that I completely forgot what my parents told me, and then it happened. *Sting!*

Our emotions can lead us down a dangerous path. And recovering from that path (whether it is sexual immorality, drug use, alcohol abuse, or whatever) isn't nearly as easy as getting over a bee sting. The long-term pain from these things can be immense, not just to ourselves, but to those around us.

The sting of our poor choices burns an imprint in our minds and creates a dark hole in our souls which cannot be filled or covered up by another affair, pill, drink, or shot. There are some things that I wish I could just erase from my mind. It was my poor decisions from the beginning that put me on the battlefield. Not that it's a mistake fighting for our country, but it could have been under different circumstances.

Sometimes life's stings aren't our fault. Mom and Dad always cherished the holidays, because it meant that their kids and grandchildren would join them in a day of memories and hope. I remember the day that Dad died and how it broke my heart that I couldn't be by his side. But the pain of losing my dad didn't sting nearly as badly as the death of our family fellowship. I knew that Dad was free from pain and at peace with our Lord and Savior Jesus Christ. I had the joy of seeing him and speaking with him as God truly changed his heart. Still, the sting from the death of family relationships loomed all around us the day we laid Daddy's worn and tired body to rest in that winter-stricken cemetery in Hinton, Oklahoma.

I miss you, Dad, and I pray that God's story in our lives can free many from the very things that entrapped us for many years. Jesus tells us that the truth will set us free and, Daddy, I am sharing the truth about our lives and how Jesus changed us.

We need to remember the stings in life and how they affected us so that we can avoid doing the same things again. I still remember throwing the rocks at the bumble bees and being chased by them down the street. I will never forget getting stung in the butt and having an allergic reaction. The bees won, and you'd think I would have given up. But I was a glutton for punishment and I went back for more. Thank God that I didn't get stung again.

My mother encouraged me to quit aggravating the bees by

giving me a little sting of her own with a switch. I was not even thinking that if one bee sent me to the doctor, what would two or three or even four stings do to me? My mother said that my body couldn't handle bee stings because of my low immune system and my being highly allergic to insect venom. She finally just told me that the bee stings could kill me.

Lots of things in life are like that. They can kill us and those around us. Maybe they can kill us physically. Or maybe they can kill our relationships, our hopes, our sense of well-being, or our will to live, and to love.

For many years, I asked God to allow me to forget many events in my life, but now I see why He allowed me to remember. As I write this book, I am in continual prayer asking God to allow His story in my life to help heal broken hearts and encourage others who have had severe life-changing injuries or have suffered from abuse, addictions, or have endured other incidents. What the bee stings in our lives have damaged, God can truly heal.

It is through the love of Jesus that individuals and families and nations can be healed and can overcome their challenges while learning to forgive those who have caused them the pain in their lives. As families, we need to be encouraged to meet on a regular basis again. This goes for our church families as well. In Hebrews 10:25, God says: "Not giving up meeting together, as some are in the habit of doing, but encouraging one another—and all the more as you see the Day approaching." Jesus knows that we need each other for encouragement, for prayer, and to help each other when help is needed.

I truly wish I could go back and not just read God's Word but apply it at each step of my life. Doing my own thing and just wanting to have what I thought was fun cost me more than I could ever imagine. I didn't know that my choices would not only sting, but they would take me on a ride I wish I never had gotten on. These rides seemed thrilling at first, but brought so much pain and suffering.

Often, I was led to the entrance of the ride by anger, hurt, or a desire to have acceptance. Ultimately, I made the final decision to get on and the sting that these choices left were much too hard to bear and left huge scars. I wanted to free myself from the sting of failure and blown opportunities such as my football and track scholarships or the opportunity to work for TWA as an airplane mechanic.

War, abuse, addiction, financial ruin and porn also led to fictitious relationships which tore my heart out. I was even ripped apart by the pain of abortion when my stripper girl-friend aborted our baby without even telling me. I would have raised that child if I had had the choice, and knowing I had lost that chance tore me up. Every choice we make affects others.

At this point in my life, I wondered when the downhill spiral was going to stop. But God knew.

Growing up in church gave me the head knowledge of Jesus Christ. But just having a head knowledge about Jesus isn't God's plan for us. He wants our whole heart and life.

I kept looking for peace and happiness in relationships based on sex and simply emotion. And I kept getting stung. Emotion tied to sexual attachment, self-gratification, and physical stimulation is a dangerous thing. It creates more damage to us and others than we can see until it's too late. If I had been living the way God wanted me to, I would not have ended up in these situations to begin with.

I was having an affair with a married woman who eventually became my first wife. If you had asked me at the time if I was a Christian, I would have told you yes. After all, I grew up in church, and I still went sometimes. But just going to church doesn't make anyone a Christian, any more than going swimming makes you a fish. Becoming a Christian involves God birthing a new spirit in us—a new heart.

Sadly, I really believed I was a Christian, and at times I may have showed some signs of being one, such as during war. But wartime religion can be like jailhouse religion. We are prone to lean on God when we are in a situation that we can't control.

We may have a head knowledge of the Bible without a true heart change in our life, truly desiring what God desires for our lives. If I would have been living for God there wouldn't have been any sexual intercourse to get me sexually, emotionally, and physically attached. And I never would have been involved with a married woman, leading her to divorce her husband and marry me.

If I could say one thing to her and her children, it is how sorry I am for the mistakes I made that deeply affected them. I am very proud of them, and I always will be. Sadly, I made the choice to do what I did instead of walking away. I am always accountable to God for my actions, but I am so thankful that Jesus placed many people in my life during that time who truly lived out who Jesus is. I started praying and seeking Him more and more, and this led me to truly accepting Jesus Christ as my Lord and Savior. Jesus became more to me than just a man in Bible stories.

There is an old saying that the longest foot in the world is from your head to your heart, and I truly believe that. I had all of the head knowledge in the world from growing up going in church. The morning that I said, "God I am yours and I want your Son Jesus Christ to lead my life," Jesus rocked my world and changed my whole life. He continues to do so daily. I have found that only He can truly heal us from the stings of life.

## CHAPTER 37

# SIDETRACKED

After I had started writing this book, I was talking to a close friend, Todd Hurley, telling him how easy it was to get sidetracked on a project like this. We laughed about it, but afterward I thought to myself, "Why does this keep happening in my life? I have the best intentions to finish the things that I start, but I tend to get sidetracked. What is causing that?"

As a Christian, I know that there is a spiritual enemy and that is Satan himself. Anything good in life comes with a price, and there is always opposition when we are trying to do something that will benefit us and someone else.

The deeper I got into writing this book, the more I came to realize the price involved in it for me. As I would write about my life, the very things I was writing about, the things God has walked me through, seemed to resurface for me. By that I mean that the pain that I went through at the time I was dealing with each challenge in life seemed to return to me. To be honest, it hurt. And I realized more than ever: blessing others means laying down our lives for them.

I wasn't writing this book so I could be healed. I was writing this book so others could find the healer and themselves be healed. But at times the writing got painful. Often, we think about the pain in our lives and we think God is doing something in us through it. Teaching us some lesson through it. And sometimes He is. But sometimes it isn't about us at all. He allows us to go through pain so that we become a blessing to others. That's what Jesus did. He went through the ultimate suffering so that we could receive the ultimate blessing. And now, if we have put our faith in Him, He lives in us. And He does the exact same thing through us. He lays down His life for others.

It would have been easy to let the pain permanently sidetrack me. We have an enemy who *wants* us to stay sidetracked, to get and stay off course. He wants to stop us from having victory in our lives, in our walk with God.

If the enemy can keep us sidetracked, he can prevent us from reaching others who need to hear our story and need our encouragement. Not only will he keep us from having freedom, peace and a fulfilling relationship with God, he wants to destroy us, our spouses, our children, extended family and friends and whomever God wants us to reach.

Writing this book had been weighing heavily on me for a while, but it wasn't until I got into another car wreck and had to have surgery again that I actually started to write it. Why did it take another back surgery to get me to surrender to the point of finally starting to write? Why does it take traumatic events to catch our attention? Why can't we just do things for the good and change for the good before these events happen?

A primary reason, I believe, is that we get sidetracked from our mission. God has given each of His children an incredible, unbelievably glorious mission. We have the privilege not only of being made one with Christ (1 Corinthians 6:17), and sharing in His life (Galatians 2:20) and His nature (2 Peter 1:4), but then of being the instruments God uses to share His life with the world. We are the ones the eternal, infinite God has chosen to live through! But we get sidetracked. It's easy, especially in this culture, to just slip into a comfortable routine. Life becomes about my comfort and pleasure. We go to church and try to be good parents and good neighbors, but the mission, the glory, is not our focus.

God's glory shines through the everyday. If I believe the Bible, then I will live out the words that God says to me. If I truly love my wife, then I will love her unconditionally, even when it hurts me to love her. If I love others, I press on through the emotional pain and finish this book. Some of them need to hear the incredible things God has done, and can do for them. I want to help them on their journey by seeing how I walked through mine and how I found hope and love in Jesus Christ, and He changed me. He is the ultimate reason that I wrote this book.

I am so thankful that Jesus did not hesitate to go to the cross for my sins. The reason He didn't get sidetracked is because He kept His eyes on His Father and continually listened to Him for directions. And He not only listened to God's directions, He followed them to the tee.

For us, wisdom is not just hearing advice from someone who has walked the walk, but applying the advice to our lives, especially if it is biblical advice.

I learned a key lesson in my military service. I learned that all of the training that we received was not in vain—even though we got aggravated with the early wake ups and at the constant screaming toward us and even having to do things that we thought were designed just to make us mad. We were learning to live life under pressure, and this meant that since we trained under pressure, we would perform under pressure. The military was renewing our minds to perform the way they wanted us to perform, and not get sidetracked.

It was easy to get sidetracked in the military if we didn't stay busy. So they kept us busy. When they didn't, someone usually started a fight among us. Why? Because we took our eye off our mission. Our mission at that time was learning to work together in situations that could end up meaning life or death.

The same thing happens in our homes and workplaces. We get off mission. We take our eyes off Jesus. If affects our abilities to be the spouses, parents, friends, or workmates we are called to be.

I was encouraged by Todd, my good friend and soldier in arms, to get busy writing again. God reminded me that we are in a war. It is a war for our souls and the souls of those around us. I want to be an effective soldier in that war. I don't want to get sidetracked.

Sometimes we need to be reminded by others not to be sidetracked. Todd did that for me. So has Heather. So has my son, Micah. Thanks to each of you for being so faithful to help me stay on track!

## CHAPTER 38

# WHAT GOES IN DOESN'T ALWAYS COME OUT

Many of us are carrying things in our lives that can create tremendous pain that will be devastating to us and to those that we love if it reappears one day. These are just like the piece of wire that the lawn mower chopped up and threw into my brother Dewayne's leg when he was eight. It's been hanging around there for many years now. If it migrated to a bad spot, it could cause him a lot of problems, decades later.

It's important to sit down and take inventory of any incidents in our lives that we never truly dealt with. Have we ever truly allowed God to deal with all of those pieces of wires in our lives? Some issues resurface later on in life and catch us by surprise. We have an enemy that would like to use these to take us out, and take out those we love.

The enemy of our soul, Satan, wants to destroy our testimony. As a Christ follower, my testimony is crucial to the credibility of who Jesus Christ is in me. If my enemy can take this away, he can render me ineffective. Whether we want to admit

WHAT GOES IN DOESN'T ALWAYS COME OUT

it or not, we have an enemy that is contending for our soul and the souls of all of those that we love dearly. He will stop at nothing to render us ineffective in our lives while trying to ultimately destroy us and all we stand for. He has learned that he can't take out God and that God's Son Jesus Christ defeated Him at the cross. His goal now is to destroy the threat of the only creation made in the image of the Creator, and that is us.

Yes, we are created in the image of God Almighty and He calls us the apple of His eye. Wow!

Is there an old wire in your life that has worked its way near to a dangerous place? The good thing is that God knows exactly where it is, and He knows exactly how to remove it.

The really awesome thing is that God even uses our wires to bring people to Him. If we had never experienced the wires in our lives, we would never know how to relate to those who are dealing with things that we have overcome through the love of Jesus Christ.

My dad had a bunch of wires in his life that he never allowed God to remove, at least not while we were growing up. One of them was pornography. A lot of people, especially men, have this wire. Half of religious men and 20 percent of religious women say that they are addicted to it. These are unbelievably high percentages. Not only was Dad's life taken out by this wire, but my exposure to it in his home growing up took me out, too, setting me up for sexual addiction later in life.

We live in a society that has become expert at shifting the blame. It's always everyone's fault except ours. But our choices deeply affect our lives and the lives of those around us. I finally learned that God was continually trying to get my attention to prevent me from destroying myself and those that I love, or even the ones that were just standing back and watching.

In the war I learned that you don't have to be next to the

incoming artillery round to be killed or maimed for life. The explosion sends out shrapnel for hundreds of feet, and it has a kill zone with at least an 80-meter radius. Think of all the families and friends that are affected by that one round.

In our homes, are we that artillery round? Are our choices taking out those living with us, or around us? I have experienced both sides of the spectrum, and I pray all the time for God to erase the memories of my many mistakes that are burned into my mind. I know that I am forgiven, and that's one of the main reasons I am writing this book. I am also writing so that you might consider the consequences that your choices are going to have on you and the ones you love. Our choices have a lifelong impact on us as well as many others.

But with God all things are possible. Healing is possible. So is change. As one of my pastors, Glynn Stone, said about pornography, "It is natural to look, but it is supernatural to not look." This is so true! The Holy Spirit living within us has brought us into the supernatural realm already, and He truly can change us.

To cooperate with God changing us, overcoming our past and our fallen world's daily influence, we have to consistently respond to God's calling on our lives. God wants us to renew our minds with His Word daily. God's Word spoken to us heals our minds from the years of corruption that have been implanted and burned into them.

Another supernatural action is to forgive. Dewayne could have blamed my dad not clearing the wire out of the yard, but he didn't. He forgave. Maybe he was too young to realize it was my dad's fault. But in any case, he didn't hold a grudge and become bitter.

If we continue to blame others for what happens to us today, we never experience the freedom that Jesus wants us to experience through forgiveness. Forgiving someone is not natural. In fact, it is supernatural—just like Jesus raising Himself from the dead and showing us that He is offering us a new life, a true relationship with the Creator of everything. Everything Jesus did for us is supernatural and comes only through the power of God. I chose the supernatural route through putting my trust and faith in Jesus Christ as my Savior. He changed me supernaturally, and He continues to rock my world.

*CHAPTER 39*

# HOWEVER YOU LEAD
# I STILL FOLLOW

I am convinced that if you believe in something, such as be-
lieving what God says in His Word, you will live it out. I
have seen over and over in my own life how I will stand up and
defend what I truly believe, such as defending our country.

I find that this comes into play most with how we spend
our time. We may find it easier to give money to God than
our time. I have learned that God wants our time, which really means He wants our lives. To really know someone, you
have to spend time with them.

For us to truly lead someone and teach them, we have to
spend time with them. This means building a relationship with
them, which builds trust and a bond. I learned more in my life
and in school and/or college from the teachers who showed
that they truly cared for me. When you become a number in
society, you become a statistic, and statistics do not show who
you are, nor do they show what or where your heart truly is.

I am saying this because our relationships are crucial to our ability to change the way we act and react to different situations in life. Our relationship with Jesus Christ transforms us from the inside out so that we can overcome the outside pressures put upon us by the world system. We have to spend time to get to know Him. When we do, He changes us to be more like Him.

The key point here is that when we spend time with someone, we start to become like them. I was spending time with my dad and becoming just like him, and in turn, he was not spending time with God. Instead, he became a reflection of our world.

When we were in Henderson, Texas, I was telling my friend, Tony Puckett, about something that Heather and I felt that God wanted us to do in our community. Though we were facing opposition, God did not tell us to quit.

Tony told me that stubbornness is a gift that simply needs to be channeled correctly. When we channel it correctly, it becomes a great asset. When I was little, I was too stubborn to not give up while learning to ride my bike, despite all my balance problems. Eventually I mastered that quest. Stubbornness has served me well as I have faced significant trials in my life.

Heather has the same gift of stubbornness. So does our son, Micah. I am blessed to have a stubborn wife, because she is too stubborn to quit in life and on me, and I thank God for her daily. The key thing about being stubborn is that we have to channel it to honor God.

Society always tries to pull us away from God's way. It strives to brainwash us and mold us into its view and its portrait of a man according to its standards. As men, we know that we are supposed to work and support our families—this is a given. But a part of the world system tells men that they can impregnate as many women as they can to prove their so-called manhood and be considered cool. But then the men are not there to raise the children that they helped bring into this world.

Being a dictator in the home and being in control of everything isn't true manhood. True manhood is allowing God to be in control of your life. The world wants to tell us that God is a crutch. Hardly. We were designed to be in relationship with God, to contain Him, and to let Him express His life through us. Fulfilling the purpose of our being is never a crutch. When we don't, we are empty inside. Then the world offers us true crutches to fill that emptiness. But they never work.

We must demonstrate compassion and outwardly express love toward our families and others. Leaning on God is not a weakness. It is a show of strength and wisdom in our lives. I leaned on my own ability for many years, and all it did was bring me down and cause me destruction.

A true man is a leader to those around him. This world often gives us a picture of a man as one who is rough and tough and controls his surroundings by any means necessary. This image makes a mockery of the purpose for which God created us in the world and in our homes.

Being a dictator isn't Christ-like. People flee nations to find freedom from dictators. Children often leave home and rebel against what they perceive as dictatorship. Some people think God acts like a dictator. But, in reality, He always has our best interest at heart, and He doesn't force us to do anything.

What God seeks is real relationship, not dictatorship.

The world system seeks complete control, and it will do anything to achieve it. It preys continually on the weak. It casts aside those who cannot produce according to its standards.

God continually tells us to follow His lead and to depend on Him for direction. God wants our full attention, and it's for our own protection. I realize that, were it not for my personal relationship with Jesus Christ, my family and I would have totally collapsed a long time ago.

Have you ever looked at an old bridge that has a huge span across water? The bridge not only has to carry its own weight, but it also carries the weight of many cars and trucks that are constantly crossing it daily. The bridge's structural support helps it carry all of that weight.

A father is designed to carry the weight of the family and support the family. We are designed to lead our family in a healthy way while keeping ourselves healthy.

As you look at a bridge, you see supports under it that are spread out evenly. God gave us His Word to support us, and He gave us the Church to encourage us and help us carry the many burdens that we pick up during our lives. Jesus is our bridge to God, and He proved to us that if we will just depend on God, not even death can keep us down.

I have learned and continue to realize more and more each day that, to be a true leader in my home, I must learn to follow. The key to a successful marriage and to being a successful father is following Jesus and living out God's Word in my life, in my home, and wherever God sends me. This is a daily process of surrendering to God.

I followed my dad's way of leading and it did not turn out well for me. I became everything that I hated in my dad growing up, and even worse. But God rocked my world and continues to change me into a reflection of His Son Jesus Christ daily. He does this by my willingness to follow Him. No one says it's is easy, and neither did Jesus. His love for us took Him to the cross on Calvary to die for our sins. Then Jesus rose from the dead, overcoming both death and the world.

My dad and I had a great conversation about two weeks before he died and went to be with Jesus. Dad asked me if I would move back to Hinton to be near him. Though Dad and I became great friends when I was an adult, I had to say to him, "I love you, Dad. But God has me in Henderson, Texas, and for the first time in my life, I truly know that I am where God wants me."

Through tears, Dad said something that shocked me: "Son, promise me that you will never change that. Promise me that you will always be where God wants you." Dad had grown old and his time to go had almost come, but God was speaking to him, and was speaking through him, no matter how old he was.

Dad learned to lead because he learned to listen and follow God, and he encouraged me to do what God wants me to do and not what my dad wanted.

Let's seek God daily and seek His direction in our lives and for our family. Then we will not mislead our loved ones into corruption.

*CHAPTER 40*

# REAL RELATIONSHIP

Through college courses and my own reading, I've learned how crucial it is for an infant to hear the voices of its parents and other caregivers even before he is born. After he is born, he also needs the touch of others for bonding and growth. The desire for relationships and to hear the voices of others, as well as to know that we are loved, has been here from the beginning of time.

As a very young child, I wanted to hear something or someone so badly that I would try anything to accomplish that. I would climb into our big stereo cabinet and lay my head onto the speaker or on the radio box. I was attracted to the light on the radio box as well as the warmth it put off.

Though I could barely hear the voices, I could feel warmth from the radio and the vibration from the speakers, and this combination kept me content and comforted. This was the next best thing to being in my mother's lap with her holding me tight and whispering into my ear. I could not always hear the words she was saying, but I could feel the warm breath and vibration enter into my ear, which let me know she was speaking directly to me. I felt the comfort and peace from her holding me tight. I was loved, and that was what mattered most.

Though I could not always hear my mother's voice, her expression of love and her willingness to do what it took to comfort me was always enough. I used to be afraid of constantly getting injections to build my low immune system up and to fight off infections. But Mom would always love me through them. It reminds me of 1 John 4:18: "There is no fear in love. But perfect love drives out fear, because fear has to do with punishment. The one who fears is not made perfect in love."

I wanted this kind of loving relationship with my dad, of course. Instead I had an abusive one. Looking back to my childhood, I struggle to remember the good times that included my dad in our home. When my son Micah was just a little baby sleeping in my lap or on my chest, I would often try to remember a time when my dad held me when I was little. Growing up, I often wondered if dad would love me enough to save me if I were dying. I have answered this question in the story about me almost drowning in a lake when I was five. He did save me. But I see now that there is a difference between saving a life and leading a life.

The struggles I've gone through have taught me many things. Among them is this: how crucial it is to tell people daily how much you love them while living it out in front of them. True love is a verb and makes a difference in the lives of others as well as our own. Heather often challenges me to show more love and affection to her and our son Micah. She also gives me hints when I am acting like my dad, and, boy, does that hit a soft spot, but it also catches my full attention.

God created us for relationship. More than anything, He created us to have a relationship with Him.

I have learned that there is a huge difference between religion and relationship. Religion is a set of rules made up by man that we have to follow or live by to be connected with God. A real relationship is what God desires with us. I deeply desired a real relationship with my father, as well as his approval. God actually fulfilled that desire for me in adulthood. But even more, he is fulfilling it in my relationship with Him. For with God all things are possible.

One night, when I was at my worst in life—literally wanting to end it—I met the Creator of the universe, and He started deleting the destructive programs that had been installed in my life. He began hitting the restart button on my life the moment I put my trust in His Son Jesus Christ.

These are three of the Bible verses that God used to speak to me during that time:

> Therefore, if anyone is in Christ, he is a new creation; old things have passed away; behold, all things have become new. (2 Corinthians 5:17, NASB)

> Jesus looked at them and said, "With man this is impossible, but with God all things are possible." (Matthew 19:26)

> "For I know the plans I have for you," declares the Lord, "plans to prosper you and not to harm you, plans to give you hope and a future." (Jeremiah 29:11)

My desire is that whoever reads this book will come to know the one true living God that I love and serve—the God of Abraham, Isaac and Jacob. I pray that you will come to know God's only Son, Jesus Christ, as your personal Savior. Of all the choices I have made in life, this choice rocked my whole world and changed me, and it continues to change me in ways that I never thought possible. My choice to live my life for Jesus has given me spiritual restoration along with changing my eternal destination. Because of my relationship with Jesus, I don't have a desire to live like I did before, and He has given me the ability to say *no* to my old ways in life, and *yes* to an entirely new way of living.

My prayer is that you will put your trust in Jesus Christ and allow Him to push the restart button in your life and upload His true peace that surpasses all understanding.

*PART THREE*

# THE PEOPLE WHO
# HELPED SHAPE ME

I want to thank my lovely wife Heather for her patience with me daily and her faithful prayers, along with her unconditional love. Heather has been such a huge encouragement to me as well as being our rock when I was too weak to stand physically and/or spiritually. I thank God daily for blessing me with her as my wife. Her faith and trust in Jesus Christ is such an encouragement to me and our son Micah. Thank you to my Honey-Bunny for all that you do, and know that I love you dearly.

Thank you, Micah, for you are such a huge blessing in my life. I am so blessed to be given a chance to love and raise a young man like you. I realize more and more every day that you are a true blessing from God above and a promise come true. Son, always remember that God keeps His promises. Always keep your eyes on God and remember that through Him all things are possible, no matter what the world may say or what you are surrounded by.

I want to thank my sister Carla Chenoweth and my two brothers, Jerry Allen and Dewayne, and Dewayne's wife, Becky, for their constant love and prayers and their consistent encouragement. I love you guys more than you will ever know. By the way, I forgive you for all the crazy stuff you did to me as we were growing up. My dear siblings, we walked many miles together in this life, and you guys are so much a part of who I am today. Your prayers are so much a part of why I am here and able to write about my life. Dewayne, I love you dearly, brother, and I am so thankful that God protected you from that gun! And thank you, Carla, for being so kind and patient with your little brothers. I love you dearly.

I want to thank my cousin Sue and her husband Josh Fogerty for their constant support in my life and for their unconditional love and encouragement. I love you guys dearly. I have been so blessed to have you as my cousin and best friend, Sue, and I am so honored to have you both as family. Sue, I was thinking back one day to Uncle Charles's reunion and those rafts we bought and played in for hours in his pool, and how every time we got together we would laugh and play as if we had never been apart. Shoot, I even remember playing together with your play cookware. We were and always will be close friends.

Sue and I always had one goal and that was/is to change the world. Sue, we can still do that with God's help by introducing people to His Son Jesus Christ.

I don't want to leave out my other cousins, because I love them all dearly: Robin and Jeff and Charlotte, Mark, Jerry Don (Pup), Dennis and Richard and many more. Robin and Jeff, I love you dearly. Thank you for being there for me.

My Aunt Kay is very special to me to this day, and so is my Aunt Karen, my dad's youngest sister. They both have been a huge inspiration to me and have been there to help me when I needed it. I pray that I can do the same for them one day. I pray regularly for my Uncle Allen, my dad's younger brother. Uncle Allen had so much talent, and I also looked up to him as I was growing up. I have never seen anyone who could sing and play like he did, and I was very proud to be his nephew. Aunt Pat, thank you for all of your encouragement that you have given and continue to give me to this day. I love all of you dearly!

I really miss going to my Grandma and Papa Brown's house regularly. I can still smell the unique smell of their pantry as I opened it up. I can see the stringed licorice now! Every time I would go and visit Grandma and Papa on leave from the army, Aunt Karen would bring me some good ol' black and red licorice if Grandma and Papa were not able to get out. Thank you very much Aunt Karen for spoiling me. I love you dearly! I miss all of our family meeting at my great grandparents' house on

Sundays after church.

To my ex-wife's parents: I am so thankful for the Christ-like example you continually lived out in front of me and for your many prayers even to this day. I will always love you guys and I am so thankful that God put you in my path.

I have been constantly encouraged by a couple of great friends whom I had the privilege of serving with in the U.S. Army while being stationed in Bamberg, West Germany, from 1988-1990 under SFC George "Chief" Warren. George was my section chief and has been such an inspiration and prayer warrior for my family and me. George, you are a true friend and brother in arms, and I love you dearly.

I will never forget the time George came to visit with my family in Henderson, Texas. My son Micah was so excited to see him, and so was I. It was such a great feeling to see him again and to see my son drawn to him like a kid to a grandpa. I am honored to have my son love him like he does. Chief, my dad would be honored for you to step in as Micah's grandpa since he has gone to be with our Lord in heaven. Chief told Micah that if he wanted to learn and be wise, he needed to close his mouth and keep his ears open. What great advice Chief gave Micah, as well as reminding me of how crucial it is to listen.

I also want to thank my dear friend and brother in arms, SPC Todd Hurley, who also served with me in Bamberg, and in the Persian Gulf War. Todd gave me a huge eye-opener when he said to me, "Curtis, I know why you're writing this book," and I responded by saying, "So do I. It's because God wants me to." Todd said, "Of course, man, but it is also because you know that you are forgiven for all the bad things you've done in your life."

Thanks, too, to my dear friend and brother in arms, James "Wolf" Worley. James, I want you to know that it was an honor to serve by your side in the Persian Gulf War. I love you, brother.

I'm so glad that my mother had contacted Judy and Henry Jordan to let them know when Wolf was flying home. Wolf flew home several weeks before me, but I was just glad that he made it home. Judy and Henry are like my adopted parents to this day and I love them more than they will ever know. Thank you, guys, for your love, friendship and many prayers that you sent up to our Father in heaven.

I can't forget Todd McGrew. Todd, you have been such an inspiration to me and such an encourager also. Thank you for your love, friendship and your faithful prayers, brother!

I am so blessed to have true friends as well as wonderful leaders like Scott Rambo and Kenny Dean at The Bridge Fellowship in Sugar Land, Texas. I was ordained and licensed by The Bridge Fellowship and I will always have a special place in my heart for this amazing church that God uses to reach many people for Jesus Christ. I am honored to be able to speak of Scott and I am so thankful for his true friendship, his constant encouragement and prayers for me and my family. Scott, I want you to know that you and your family and church family are loved dearly and prayed for regularly. I am thankful for Scott's willingness to follow God and not the crowd.

Heather and I are so blessed to have Roger and Charlene Dauzat from The Bridge as prayer warriors on our behalf. Roger, I truly consider you to be a second dad to me. I love you guys more than I can say.

My thanks go as well to Chaplain May and his wife Cheryl. I want to thank them for their many prayers and true friendship throughout these years. I was truly honored to have Chaplain May say the prayer at my ordination.

God is so faithful to consistently place us where we need to be at specific times in our lives when we allow Him to do so. God blessed us in East Texas by allowing us to worship and grow closer to Him at Mobberly Baptist Church in Longview, Texas. I was encouraged daily by our leadership at Mobberly and I am truly grateful for their dedication to our Lord and Savior Jesus Christ and for their hearts for broken people.

We love you guys in the LaJoie class and always will and we are so thankful for the time that God allowed us to fellowship and serve together while He had us at Mobberly. I want to say a special thanks to Jay Shepherd for his constant support, love and prayers and for being a true friend. Thanks to Shawn Smith, Sr., for all of your prayers. Shawn Jr., your friendship means so much to me. I love ya, bro!

Thank you, Tony Puckett, for your true friendship and many prayers for our family and thank you for giving us the Honda Pilot that we needed badly. I will forever be grateful for your kindness and love for me and my family. I am truly honored to call you my brother, my friend, and my mentor.

Tony is a great communicator whom I love to hear speak on marriage and the family. He loves God and loves family. If you are ever in Longview, Texas, you might want to look him up, or if you are having struggles in your marriage, I would encourage you to contact him.

I want to say a special thank you to Michael and Teresa Chaloner for their consistent prayers and encouragement and putting up with me as I grew up. And to Lee Norton and Bruce Price for always tolerating me in Sunday school! You both have been such an inspiration to me.

Lee was a fellow brother-in-arms and U.S. Army soldier. He reminded me of a verse on Sunday, December 29, 2014. I was dearly blessed by God that day as He allowed me to speak at the First Baptist Church of Hinton, Oklahoma in their awesome new sanctuary. This is the church I grew up attending. I was so blessed to have so many great people at FBC Hinton who loved God and invested in my life. Lee, who was one of them, had a verse printed on the war veterans memorial in Hinton. John 15:13 says, "There is no greater love than this: that a person would lay down his life for the sake of his friends" (ABPE). Lee, I want you to know that your true friendship has had a huge effect on my life. You were not only a patient and forgiving teacher of mine when I was growing up, you were also and are a dear friend.

One of things I remember most about Lee occurred when I came back to the U.S. after serving two and a half years in Bamberg, West Germany. When I was returned, I applied for auto insurance. I was told that since I had gone without insurance for over two years that it was going to be over two thousand dollars. I had been serving our country in the military and I had not been driving in Europe, so why would I have needed insurance? Lee stepped in and rescued me. Lee put me on his policy so that I could afford the insurance. That way, when six months was up I could prove that I had carried insurance on my vehicle, and my insurance would be the normal price again.

Thank you, Lee, for all you have done for me and for our country. I would also like to thank you for the continued encouragement even today. The hug and tears that we shared after the message God put on my heart to share at my home church, FBC of Hinton, will be imprinted on my heart and mind for the rest of my life. I love you, man, and never forget that.

I want to thank my lifelong friend, Myron Hulet, for his support and encouragement throughout this journey. Thank you, brother, for being there to lift me up when I needed to be lifted and scolding me when I needed correction. I will always cherish the many days that we spent together growing up, from

riding mini-bikes to building underground forts and tree hous-
es. We had a blast! I can't forget the BB gun fights, but that is
another story in itself. Myron is the owner of Texas Flight in
Tomball, Texas. If you want to learn to fly, have your plane
serviced or worked on or just go up for an afternoon flight,
please look him up. You will not be disappointed! I love you,
my friend and my brother.

David, my childhood best friend, was always there for me.
David is a good example of us not being guaranteed a long life.
When David died it broke my heart because I was not able
to be there with him during his illness or during his passing.
Though the sting of death was there, I am comforted now by
knowing that he knew Jesus Christ as his personal Savior.

I am so blessed to be back in contact with some of the kids
that I played with and went to church with in Shore Acres. It is
exciting to know that Virgil Walters is a pastor now in Missis-
sippi and that his brother Richard is a Christ follower who has
overcome many heart issues. We still joke about how we would
literally fight over who was going to sit on the ice cream maker
and crank.

Nola Crick, I want you to know that you have been a huge
inspiration to me. You have always been there to encourage me
and cheer me on. I still have that awesome photo album that
you made from the newspaper clippings and pictures of my senior year. I want to thank you from the bottom of my heart for
all of your encouragement, prayers, and for being such a good
friend. I love you and your entire family very much, Nola!

Quetta, I love you with all my heart and you will always be
family to me. Thank you for the friend you were to my momma.

I will never forget another close friend of Mom's, Ruby Pow-
ers, who always made me cookies as a child. I have always loved

Ruby dearly. She was there with me outside of Mom and Dad's house until almost four o'clock in the morning the night Mom died, praying with me, hugging me and just comforting me. Thank you, Ruby, for the cookies that you always brought me in the Pringles can and thank you for being my rock the night that my mother went to be with Jesus.

I also want to thank Chaplain Milton (Chap) and his wife Cheryl for your love, prayers and encouragement. I love you guys!

SFC K, I truly understand now what you were saying. Thank you for all you taught me before and during the war.

Jeanie, thank you for your friendship to this day. I have and always will see you as my sister and I love and miss you, Janell, and your mom Peggy.

Coach Brack and Mrs. Chaloner, I will never forget your many prayers and constant encouragement and, of course, your smiling faces. Michael Chaloner, thank you for all of your tolerance, patience, and encouragement and your many prayers for me. I am blessed to have you as a brother in Christ and friend to this day.

Coach Lewis, I want you to know that you encouraged me more than you will ever know and still do. I love you, coach, and I thank you for your many prayers throughout the years.

Dr. Lambeth, I want to thank you for your guidance, care and friendship. I love you, my brother, and I am so grateful to our God for leading me to you.

Mrs. Rodgers, I am so blessed to have had you as my teacher and even more blessed to have you as my friend. Thank you for all of your encouragement back in kindergarten and even today. I love you dearly and may God continue to bless you.

Thank you, Anthony, for your encouragement and for always finding the good in me. I am honored to be your friend to this day and I look forward to working with you and helping others together one day.

Curt, thank you for your encouragement, help, and advice and especially for your friendship. I know that God has many more miles for us to travel together on His behalf and I am looking forward to it. I love you, brother.

Dr. Malik encouraged me to write this book. I am honored to have him as a doctor and a friend. I would recommend him anywhere, anytime because he is the most caring and competent neurosurgeon in this country in my book.

I want to thank Dr. Sasha Kecman at Kecman Chiropractic in Henderson, Texas for his care, friendship and encouragement during this journey. If you are in East Texas please look him up. He can help you on your journey to improve your life.

To my family, I love you guys, and we have had some great times together. I hope for many more fun times. Remember that in order for us to have fun times, we have to get together. We never know if we have tomorrow, and we need to live like there is no tomorrow!

*PART FOUR*

# THE FACTS

# OPIOID ADDICTION
# FACTS AND FIGURES

The following are taken from the American Society of Addiction Medicine's fact sheet entitled "2016 Opioid Addiction Facts and Figures." The figures continue to grow worse by the year.

- Opioids are a class of drugs that include the illicit drug heroin as well as the licit prescription pain relievers oxycodone, hydrocodone, codeine, morphine, fentanyl and others.
- Of the 20.5 million Americans 12 or older that had a substance use disorder in 2015, 2 million had a substance use disorder involving prescription pain relievers and 591,000 had a substance use disorder involving heroin.
- Drug overdose is the leading cause of accidental death in the US, with 52,404 lethal drug overdoses in 2015. Opioid addiction is driving this epidemic, with 20,101 overdose deaths related to prescription pain relievers, and 12,990 overdose deaths related to heroin in 2015.

- From 1999 to 2008, overdose death rates, sales and substance use disorder treatment admissions related to prescription pain relievers increased in parallel. The overdose death rate in 2008 was nearly four times the 1999 rate; sales of prescription pain relievers in 2010 were four times those in 1999; and the substance use disorder treatment admission rate in 2009 was six times the 1999 rate.

- In 2012, 259 million prescriptions were written for opioids, which is more than enough to give every American adult their own bottle of pills.

- In 2015, 276,000 adolescents were current nonmedical users of pain reliever, with 122,000 having an addiction to prescription pain relievers.

- People often share their unused pain relievers, unaware of the dangers of nonmedical opioid use. Most adolescents who misuse prescription pain relievers are given them for free by a friend or relative.

- The prescribing rates for prescription opioids among adolescents and young adults nearly doubled from 1994 to 2007.

- Women are more likely to have chronic pain, be prescribed prescription pain relievers, be given higher doses, and use them for longer time periods than men. Women may become dependent on prescription pain relievers more quickly than men.

- 48,000 women died of prescription pain reliever overdoses between 1999 and 2010. Prescription pain reliever overdose deaths among women increased more than 400% from 1999 to 2010, compared to 237% among men.

# PRESCRIPTION DRUG SIDE EFFECTS

The following are lists of side effects from the drugs I was on for a span of 18 years. These side effects are real. I have experienced many of them myself.

I have been off of all medications, including aspirin and Tylenol, for almost three years now and I feel better than I have in years. I mentioned in Chapter 40 various things that have been very beneficial to my recovery and staying healthy and feeling good once again. Eastern medicine, such as massage therapy and acupuncture, along with a proper diet, supplements and exercise have been extremely effective in controlling my chronic pain and has eliminated it for the most part. This Far Eastern approach has also eliminated the PTSD/anxiety and depression. In addition, it has eliminated the cravings that I had from being addicted to narcotics and psychotropic medications for most of two decades. I encourage people to research and make sure practitioners truly practice Far Eastern methods.

Proper supplements such as magnesium, Gaba and 5HTP can help encourage the brain to start producing or increasing its production of serotonin, which is the body's natural feel good hormone. This hormone controls our moods and even how our body responds to stress and pain.

I encourage you to look and read the side effects of *any* medications that you are on. Medications were designed to help us over a hump in life, but not to become a lifestyle for us. Here are the side effects of the medications I was on:

### Ativan (for anxiety disorders)

*Common side effects:* sedation, dizziness, weakness, and unsteadiness

*Less common side effects:* fatigue, drowsiness, amnesia, memory impairment, confusion, disorientation, depression, unmasking of depression, disinhibition, euphoria, suicidal ideation/attempt, ataxia, asthenia, extrapyramidal symptoms, convulsions/seizures, tremor, vertigo, eye function/visual disturbance (including diplopia and blurred vision), dysarthria/slurred speech, change in libido, impotence, decreased orgasm; headache, coma; respiratory depression, apnea, worsening of sleep apnea, worsening of obstructive pulmonary disease; gastrointestinal symptoms including nausea, change in appetite, constipation, jaundice, increase in bilirubin, increase in liver transaminases, increase in alkaline phosphatase; hypersensitivity reactions, anaphylactoid reactions; dermatological symptoms, allergic skin reactions, alopecia; hyponatremia; thrombocytopenia, agranulocytosis, pancytopenia; hypothermia; and autonomic manifestations (Source: rxlist.com)

### Bellatal / belladonna alkaloids and phenobarbital (for irritable bowel syndrome and ulcers)

*Common side effects:* Constipation, decreased sweating, dizziness, dry mouth, nose, throat, or skin

*Less common or rare side effects:* Bloated feeling, blurred vision, decreased flow of breast milk, difficult urination, difficulty in swallowing, headache, increased sensitivity of eyes to sunlight, loss of memory, nausea or vomiting, unusual tiredness or weakness (Source: drugs.com)

### Demerol HCI / Meperidine (an opioid pain medication, a narcotic)

*Common side effects:* lightheadedness, dizziness, sedation, nausea, vomiting, and sweating.

*Less common side effects:* Mood changes (e.g., euphoria, dysphoria), weakness, headache, agitation, tremor, involuntary muscle movements (e.g., muscle twitches, myoclonus), severe convulsions, transient hallucinations and disorientation, confusion, delirium, visual disturbances, Dry mouth, constipation, biliary tract spasm, flushing of the face, tachycardia, bradycardia, palpitation, hypotension, syncope, Urinary retention, Pruritus, urticaria, other skin rashes, anaphylaxis (Source: rxlist.com)

### Effexor (for depression, anxiety, and panic)

*More common side effects:* Lack or loss of strength, severe headache, sweating

*Less common side effects:* Blurred vision, chest pain, fast or irregular heartbeat, mood or mental changes, ringing or buzzing in the ears, suicidal thoughts (Source: drugs.com)

### Fentanyl (an opioid pain medication, a narcotic)

*Common side effects:* fever, respiratory depression, nausea, vomiting, and diaphoresis

*Other side effects:* hypoventilation (Source: drugs.com)

### Gabapentin (an anti-epileptic or anticonvulsant)

*Common side effects:* ataxia, dizziness, drowsiness, fatigue, fever, nystagmus, sedated state, and viral infection

*Other side effects:* blurred vision, diplopia, peripheral edema, tremor, amblyopia, irritability, and xerostomia (Source: drugs. com)

**Methadone (for withdrawal symptoms from narcotics; methadone is also a narcotic)**
*Common side effects:* lightheadedness, dizziness, sedation, nausea, vomiting, and sweating.

*Less common side effects:* asthenia (weakness), edema, headache, arrhythmias, bigeminal rhythms, bradycardia, cardiomyopathy, ECG abnormalities, extrasystoles, flushing, heart failure, hypotension, palpitations, phlebitis, QT interval prolongation, syncope, T-wave inversion, tachycardia, torsades de pointes, ventricular fibrillation, ventricular tachycardia, agitation, confusion, disorientation, dysphoria, euphoria, insomnia, hallucinations, seizures, visual disturbances, hypogonadism, abdominal pain, anorexia, biliary tract spasm, constipation, dry mouth, glossitis, reversible thrombocytopenia has been described in opioid addicts with chronic hepatitis, hypokalemia, hypomagnesemia, weight gain, antidiuretic effect, urinary retention or hesitancy, amenorrhea, reduced libido and/ or potency, reduced ejaculate volume, reduced seminal vesicle and prostate secretions, decreased sperm motility, abnormalities in sperm morphology, pulmonary edema, respiratory depression, pruritus, urticaria, other skin rashes, and rarely, hemorrhagic urticaria (Source: rxlist.com)

**Methocarbamol (a muscle relaxant)**
*Side effects:* Anaphylactic reaction, angioneurotic edema, fever, headache, Bradycardia, flushing, hypotension, syncope, thrombophlebitis, Dyspepsia, jaundice, nausea and vomiting, Leukopenia, Hypersensitivity reactions, Amnesia, confusion, diplopia, dizziness or lightheadedness, drowsiness,

insomnia, mild muscular incoordination, nystagmus, sedation, seizures (including grand mal), vertigo, Blurred vision, conjunctivitis, nasal congestion, metallic taste, pruritus, rash, urticaria (Source: rxlist.com)

**Norco (an opioid, or narcotic, pain medication consisting of acetaminophen and hydrocodone)**

*Common side effects:* lightheadedness, dizziness, sedation, nausea and vomiting.

*Less common side effects:* Drowsiness, mental clouding, lethargy, impairment of mental and physical performance, anxiety, fear, dysphoria, psychic dependence, mood changes, constipation, Ureteral spasm, spasm of vesical sphincters, urinary retention, skin rash, pruritus, allergic reactions, thrombocytopenia, agranulocytosis. (Source: rxlist.com)

**Oxycontin/Oxycodone (an opioid pain medication, a narcotic)**

*Common side effects:* Constipation, nausea, somnolence, dizziness, pruritus, vomiting, dry mouth, asthenia, and sweating

*Less common side effects:* abdominal pain, diarrhea, dyspepsia, gastritis, chills, fever, anorexia, twitching, abnormal dreams, anxiety, confusion, dysphoria, euphoria, insomnia, nervousness, thought abnormalities, dyspnea, hiccups, skin rash, postural hypotension (Source: rxlist.com)

Prozac (for depression, OCD, panic)

*Common side effects:* Hives, itching, or skin rash, inability to sit still, restlessness

*Less common side effects:* Chills or fever, joint or muscle pain Source: drugs.com)

## Soma Compound (aspirin and Carisoprodol, a muscle relaxant)

*Common side effects:* Burning feeling in the chest or stomach, indigestion, stomach upset, tenderness in the stomach area

*Less common side effects:* Cough, difficult or troubled breathing, large, hive-like swelling on the face, eyelids, lips, tongue, throat, hands, legs, feet, or sex organs, noisy breathing, shakiness and unsteady walk, shortness of breath, tightness in the chest, unsteadiness, trembling, or other problems with muscle control or coordination (Source: drugs.com)

## Trazodone (an anti-depressant)

*Common side effects:* blurred vision, dizziness, drowsiness, headache, nausea, vomiting, and xerostomia

*Other side effects:* syncope, edema, ataxia, confusion, diarrhea, hypotension, insomnia, sedated state, and tachycardia (Source: drugs.com)

## Valium (for anxiety)

*Common side effects:* drowsiness, tired feeling, dizziness, spinning sensation, fatigue, constipation, ataxia (loss of balance), memory problems, restlessness, irritability, muscle weakness, nausea, drooling, dry mouth, slurred speech, blurred or double vision, skin rash, itching, or loss of interest in sex (Source: rxlist.com)

## Venlafaxine (an antidepressant)

*Common side effects:* anorgasmia, asthenia, constipation, dizziness, drowsiness, insomnia, nausea, nervousness, headache, anorexia, decreased appetite, delayed ejaculation, diaphoresis, and xerostomia

*Other side effects:* abdominal pain, anxiety, blurred vision, hypertension, impotence, tremor, visual disturbance, vomiting, diarrhea, dyspepsia, increased serum cholesterol, pharyngitis, vasodilatation, weight loss, decreased libido, increased dream activity, yawning, abnormal dreams, and flatulence (Source: drugs.com)

**Wellbutrin/Bupropion (an antidepressant)**
*Common side effects:* insomnia, nausea, pharyngitis, weight loss, constipation, dizziness, headache, and xerostomia
*Other side effects:* abdominal pain, agitation, arthralgia, chest pain, migraine, skin rash, urinary frequency, anxiety, asthenia, confusion, diarrhea, hostility, hypertension, lack of concentration, myalgia, nervousness, palpitations, pruritus, tinnitus, tremor, vomiting, anorexia, diaphoresis, dysgeusia, flushing, and abnormal dreams (Source: drugs.com)

*PART FIVE*

# TRIBUTES TO CURTIS BROWN AND PRAISE FOR *GOD IS BIGGER*

I have been truly blessed by getting to know Curtis Brown and reading his book. One of my legislative priorities is helping our Veterans with Traumatic Brain Injury (TBI) and Post Traumatic Stress Disorder (PTSD). Curtis has been miraculously healed from severe childhood trauma and PTSD and shares his compelling story about his journey to well-being and becoming a dynamic and living model of what God can do with an individual who gives his life to Christ. Curtis was doomed to self-destruction because of his upbringing and then what happened to him physically, mentally and emotionally in his military duty in Operation Desert Storm. Perhaps, most importantly, is the life-changing transformation he made from the numerous psychotropic drugs he was placed on by the doctors and psychiatrists in the VA system. These drugs were, in fact, killing him until he found the Lord, which saved his life and gave him the strength to "right his own ship" and then the awesome opportunity to help and bless so many others with his faith and personal example. Curtis has been healed in every way, and he lives today to share this testimony with everyone he comes in contact with, from the desperation of living with PTSD and ending his life to be the bright and shining light to those who are suffering the same as he did, and giving them hope through Christ for their lives. I am truly blessed to know this man and know his story as he humbly presents it in this compelling book!

STATE REPRESENTATIVE RICK MILLER,
Texas House District 26

Dear Curtis,

Congratulations on getting your book published. Precious few have had the courage to write about their challenges, trials and tribulations associated with their own experiences as you now have. Post Traumatic Syndrome Disorder (PTSD) is real! When coupled with prescription pain medication addictions and the onset of depression, many cannot cope and reverse their path as you have.

You have written an excellent book that should raise lots of eyebrows. Of course, much of your subject matter was about your own devastating, tumultuous and hard-fought experiences. Many who read this book will identify with you and all that you have endured. You have done a wheelbarrow-full of research, soul searching, praying and ministering to others on this subject. I admire you.

With the growing number of daily veteran suicides, I pray that your experiences shared within these words will save many. If this book saves only one life, then you have lived up to God's calling to write it.

I applaud you and will say, I am so thankful for the many afternoons and evenings we have spent together over the last 17 years. If not for you, I very easily could have been one of those lost.

> RICH ROGERS, Combat veteran CW3 Retired,
> Attack Helicopter Instructor Pilot

My prayer is that this book and Curtis' journey with the Lord through many struggles will encourage your heart and give you hope. God can do anything! Curtis is proof!

> JAN LAJOIE, Mobberly Baptist Church

Curtis Brown proves that God loves making trades. I've personally watched God trade Curtis' grief for joy, bondage for freedom, ashes for beauty, and death for life. You will be amazed at the trials, suffering and sorrow that Curtis has endured, but you'll also be drawn to know and experience his Heavenly Father, the great trade maker, more deeply.

KENNY DEAN, Palladium Campus Pastor, The Bridge Fellowship of Sugar Land

I have heard his stories of courage in the military. I have been speechless as I looked at the x-rays of his neck and back. I have watched him overcome medications that enslaved him as he dealt with constant pain. However, the greatest thing that I have witnessed was watching Curtis and Heather fight Hell to save their marriage. My prayer is that this book will encourage you to fight Hell as well.

TONY PUCKETT, Mobberly Baptist Church

In the world where substance abuse has become standard procedure for enduring traumatic injury, Curtis Brown redirects the flawed philosophy that we are left hopeless and without a more productive means of lasting recovery. His simple, yet profound, approach to developing an authentic relationship with Jesus Christ testifies to the validity of relationship over religion. The natural fellowship that arose from nurturing his bond with a loving God is evident not only in his humility, but through his own outpouring of love and service towards those struggling with Post Traumatic Stress (PTS), Traumatic Brain Injury (TBI), clinical depression and addictions. His book re-emphasizes our need to exchange man's knowledge for God's wisdom. It teaches that we're no longer slaves forced to live in a spirit of fear, but disciples, free to live and grow in God's grace.

JENNY REESE CLARK, Author/Testimonial Speaker

I've known Curtis Brown and his family for almost ten years. From the first time he and I met, we clicked. His love for people was very evident. He loved the Lord and was bold about sharing it. As a staff member at his church this kind of commitment excited me.

Through the years, I've watched Curtis's body ravage him with crippling pain and life handing him one disappointment after another and yet, he still boasted about the sustaining nature of his Savior. He still sang praises of joy because his body was not supposed to let him walk, yet he was walking. The surgeries, medications, and even family difficulties didn't choke his joy or his pursuit of what God wanted him to do.

I'm thrilled that you are about to read his story. It's a fantastic culmination of all that he's encountered. I count it an honor to know Curtis. He's an inspiration to me and after reading his book, I know you to will be moved and changed as well.

JAY SHEPHERD, Minister of Outreach/
Assimilation, Mobberly Baptist Church

I am honored to have been given a chance to tell you how much I think of my awesome lifelong friend Curtis Brown. From excursions in Red Rock Canyon, through the hijinks of our school days, to recently getting to hear him preach, Curtis has been an inspiration to me and has repeatedly impressed me over the years.

Local heroes all too often go unnoticed, but getting to hear Curtis preach proved to me that his mission here on earth did not end with his military service. His broad shoulders have yet again undertaken an overwhelming task and he has once again proven himself to be dependable, trustworthy, and to show unfailing love. He genuinely loves people, works hard, and projects a warm, cheerful attitude. Furthermore, he tries to lift the spirits of those around him, and he reaches out to help people in need.

Since returning from military service, Curtis has put in endless hours working to help improve veteran benefits and to help those struggling with PTSD and depression. He offers hope in the darkness, and love for the hurting. And although he received significant injuries during his military service, he still moves forward, through the pain, inspiring many.

He is a true humanitarian and is the very epitome of a hero because he is noble, self-sacrificing, and takes on enormous challenges. He fights valiantly through the tough times and leans on God when he feels he can no longer handle the tasks before him. God lifts him up, brushes him off, gives him a hug, and he keeps on going.

And in reflecting the love of God to others, Curtis has recently even helped shine that light of love to me personally when I was going through a really tough time in my life. Curtis reminded me that life is a battle, but that victory is possible, and I cannot express the depths of my gratitude, nor the heights of my respect for my dear and close friend Curtis. Because God is in his heart, Curtis shines characteristics that represent all that is good in our world. My heart is warmed, and I am thankful to God that he is my friend.

WADE PRICE


I met Curtis Brown about four years ago. At that time, I was a broadcast news reporter, and he was man with a story involving his complaints with Veterans Affairs. For my editors, he was a story. To me, his story was a side note to what I was seeing before me—a man losing health and function, a family strained by life, and a blonde young man who loved his parents and wanted the carefree life of a child.

I also appreciate seeing when a young man is devoted to his father. I saw that four years ago, as young Micah cherished his father Curtis. As Curtis tried to tell me about the struggles of his life, the things that fill the pages of this book, I saw Micah reveal—in his grabbing of Curtis's hands and his interruptions of dad's speaking— that every second with his family was precious and precarious.

I haven't seen Micah in more than a year, I believe. I've talked to Curtis and can hear in his voice that so many of the domestic, addictive or destructive moments of his family's life have turned a corner. I hear the words of Christ in Curtis's testimony, and I believe that Micah's crucial moments of love and support from his full family are still precious but not so precarious. I believe it's possible only because Curtis continued—without a second of failure—to believe in God's promises, that his family could be healed, and that his family was foremost in this life.

JIMMY ISAAC


I have known Curtis now for nearly seven years. The more that I got to know Curtis, the more I could see what a deep, close, and very personal relationship this man has with God. It became very apparent to me that God brought us together. I have never met a person that I can honestly say is not afraid to witness to anyone for Jesus Christ. It doesn't matter what the circumstance at that very moment or the location whether public or private. Curtis loves to share the Gospel with anyone, believer or nonbeliever. It doesn't take long to see being around him that the love of God is in him. His actions convey everything that he speaks. He is truly an amazing man of God. I wondered to myself on many occasions how this man could be on fire so passionately for God. It wasn't until the day that Curtis shared with me his personal testimony that I fully understood where that passion came from. I sat in awe as I listened to him tell me of his childhood, family life, and experience in the United States Army. What an amazing story. The best part about a person sharing their testimony is hearing the outcome. I believe what has amazed me the most is hearing and seeing for myself the other end of all those hurtful events in his life. I have seen the man that God took him from being, to the man of God that the Lord Himself propelled Curtis to become and the amazing ministry that God has given to him. I have never known anyone else personally who conveys what living life as a Christian example should be or comes as close to as Curtis Brown.

God has blessed this man in so many ways by giving him an amazing family, a fantastic church home, and a ministry that has given him the ability to speak to untold numbers of people all across the United States and foreign countries. I have personally seen him witness the love of Jesus Christ while being in some of the hardest times in his life to men and women at a nearby veterans' hospital, desperately in need of hearing the Gospel and knowing Jesus Christ personally.

I have seen Curtis in the best of times and the worst of times. The one thing that has always—and I do mean always—remained consistent is his love and passion for Jesus Christ, for sharing His Gospel, and living his life on this earth to the best of his ability to be the example of what it means to live the Christian life. If there was ever a person that I would want as my friend or to speak to others about Christ, it would be Curtis Brown. His story and testimony are meant to convey a message of where God found him and where he found God. It is a story of triumph and heartbreak where God found a broken man and put him back together to share that story so that the Lord could be glorified because of it. I encourage you to visit with Curtis and to give him the opportunity to share his story with you and that of your congregation. Thank you for this opportunity to tell you about an awesome man of God.

MICHAEL HUNT

# CONTACT THE AUTHOR

Curtis R. Brown is a disabled Persian Gulf Veteran who served in the U.S. Army from 1988-1992 and currently resides in Texas with his wife of thirteen years, Heather, their twelve-year-old son, Micah, and a spoiled rotten English bulldog. In addition to serving in the army, Curtis served in both the Oklahoma and Texas National Guards for a total of four years.

In addition to authoring, Curtis hosts the radio show "Battlefield Connections with Curtis Brown." The shows airs on KKHT, 100.7 FM at 10:30 a.m. Sundays and also on IHeart radio.

Curtis also speaks at churches and other venues with transparency and hope on dysfunctional family life, abuse, PTSD, addiction, chronic pain and more.

*God Is Bigger: His Amazing Rescue from Abuse, Addiction, PTSD, Divorce, and Despair* is Curtis's first book and is available on Amazon and through bookstores.

For bulk book orders or to schedule a speaking engagement, you can contact Curtis at: speaking@curtisbrown.org.

Made in the USA
Middletown, DE
30 May 2019